THE SEED OF MADNESS

*Constitution, Environment,
and Fantasy in the Organization
of the Psychotic Core*

THE SEED OF MADNESS

*Constitution, Environment,
and Fantasy in the Organization
of the Psychotic Core*

Edited by

Vamık D. Volkan

and

Salman Akhtar

INTERNATIONAL UNIVERSITIES PRESS
Madison   Connecticut

INTERNATIONAL UNIVERSITIES PRESS and International Universities Press, Inc. (& design) ® are registered trademarks of International Universities Press, Inc.

Library of Congress Cataloging-in-Publication Data

The seed of madness : constitution, environment, and fantasy in the organization of the psychotic core / edited by Vamık Volkan and Salman Akhtar.
    p.   cm.
   Includes bibliographical references and index.
   ISBN 0-8236-6023-0
   1. Psychoses—Etiology. 2. Psychology, Pathological. I. Volkan, Vamık D., 1932–   II. Akhtar, Salman, 1946 July 31–
RC512.S43 1997   96-25084
                                                  CIP

To
John Kafka

Clinician, Theoretician,
Colleague, and Friend

CONTENTS

ACKNOWLEDGMENTS

Some of the chapters in this book were originally presented at the eleventh International Symposium for the Psychotherapy of Schizophrenia, Washington, DC, June 12, 1994. Others were written specifically for this volume by individuals distinguished in the study of overt or dormant psychotic processes. First and foremost, therefore, we are grateful to the organizers of the International Symposium. Second, we are grateful to the colleagues who gave their thought, time, and effort to this undertaking. We are also thankful to Bruce Edwards (Managing Editor), Carole Hamilton (Editor), and Kelly Hale (Administrative Assistant) at the Center for the Study of Mind and Human Interaction for their editorial assistance. Finally, we wish to thank Maryann Nevin who prepared the manuscript of this book with outstanding skill and patience.

CONTRIBUTORS

Salman Akhtar, M.D. Professor of Psychiatry, Jefferson Medical College; Training and Supervising Analyst, Philadelphia Psychoanalytic Institute, Philadelphia, Pennsylvania.

Maurice Apprey, Ph.D. Professor of Psychiatry and Associate Dean, Minority Affairs, University of Virginia School of Medicine, Charlottesville, Virginia.

Gabriele Ast, M.D. Private practice of psychoanalysis, Munich, Germany; formerly associated with Ludwig Maximilian University, Munich, Germany.

L. Bryce Boyer, M.D. Co-Director, Center for the Advanced Study of Psychoses, San Francisco; Director, Boyer Research Institute, Berkeley, California.

Johannes Lehtonen, M.D. Professor and Chairman, Department of Psychiatry, University and the University Hospital of Kuopio, Finland; Training and Supervising Analyst, Finnish Psychoanalytic Institute.

Simo Salonen, M.D. Training and Supervising Analyst, Finnish Psychoanalytic Institute; currently in private practice, Turku, Finland.

Vamık Volkan, M.D. Professor of Psychiatry and Director, Center of the Study of Mind and Human Interaction, University of Virginia, Charlottesville, Virginia; Training and Supervising Analyst, Washington Psychoanalytic Institute; Editor, *Mind and Human Interaction.*

Part One

Laying the Groundwork

The Seed of Madness

Vamik D. Volkan, M.D.

The aim of this book is to study the beginning of madness. My focus in this chapter is on how a "mad seed" develops as well as how it differs from a "normal" core. Even though many investigators currently reduce the study of madness to biological formulations concerning genes, biochemistry, and brain anatomy, it remains important not to overlook the psychological components in the formation of the seed of madness. To do so would be comparable to assessing a painting simply according to the chemical compositions of the paints used to create the artistic effect. The importance of the psychological factors in the beginning of madness therefore need to be reviewed and updated.

Recent research on infants, such as that conducted by Emde (1988a,b) and Greenspan (1989), reemphasizes what earlier researchers into infancy, such as Spitz (1957, 1965) and Mahler (1968), have shown, and observed again and again in clinical work. It indicates that in spite of psychobiological activities and potentials, the infant mind "hatches," becoming more mature and cohesive when mother–child experiences function as its "incubator." Such interaction provides a symbolic channel for the start of a self that is originally undifferentiated. It is my belief that the nature of this channel, as well as the ingredients that pass through it, determine whether the seed will be "normal" and evolving, or "mad" and fixated.

No doubt we will learn much more from further research regarding the infant's psychobiological potentials and the details of the mother–child interactions that activate them. However, aspects of what happens in these interactions—for example, the mother's *unconscious* fantasies about her infant and later, the developing child's *unconscious* fantasies about him (or her) self, his mother, and life in general—will remain covert, and hence not subject to measurable research (Apprey, 1993). Clinical work with patients remains necessary in order to "reconstruct" the meaning of undifferentiated and subsequently poorly differentiated early mother–child experiences.

Early Mother–Child Experiences

The term *channel* is used for something that, in reality, cannot be observed or clearly described. We have no choice but to refer to metaphors in conceptualizing the early mother–child experience, and with the channel analogy we can begin looking at various issues in more complicated and sophisticated ways. What passes through the channel includes genetic (biological) determinants; the intensity of drive derivatives, including affects; growth-stimulating and growth-inhibiting external influences that echo internally; fixation-producing traumas; interference with transitional objects and phenomena; various ego and later, superego identifications; cultural and educational variables; unconscious fantasies of both the mother and child; and congruence between the mother's activity and temperament and those of the child. These factors influence one another and mingle as they pass through the channel, and all appear in the context of the mother–child interactions. The strength and stability of such interactions makes for either a smooth flow or for an incompatible mixture.

Initially, as the components flow through the channel, biology and psychology (body and mind) are basically undifferentiated. When the seed of the self is established, undifferentiated at first from the images of the object (mother), it does not immediately become crystallized, but does eventually jell. It becomes a structure with "backbone" when the ego mechanisms associated with it distinguish self-images and representations from object images and representations, and integrate libidinally and aggressively invested self-images and representations. Now cohesive, the self is associated with more mature ego functions, and we say that the development of the core is "normal." If, however, the seed of self has not evolved, but remains undifferentiated or poorly differentiated and associated only with *primitive* ego mechanisms, we say that it is fixated as an infantile psychotic self, a "seed of madness."

The Primitive Ego Functions

The primitive ego functions that I am interested in here refer primarily to two cycles of self and object relationships. The first cycle is the cycle of *fusion-defusion*. This occurs when the self-image is not differentiated from the object image (fusion). When a differentiation occurs (defusion), it is only temporary and unstable. The differentiated self soon has to fuse with the same or another object representation to complete the cycle. For example, a patient sitting on a chair reports that he *is* the chair. Then he asks "Who am I?" as his representation defuses from the image of the chair. After a while, he sits on a couch and declares he *is* the couch.

The second cycle is called the *introjective–projective cycle*. Here, the self representation is differentiated in a stable way, however poorly, from the object representation. Aspects of the self representation, however, are projected into the object representation. Then, the projected elements as well as aspects of the object representation are introjected. The cycle continues at a quick pace. *Introjective–projective cycle* is a term that covers various forms of introjections and projections, including projective identification. A patient sits on a chair and knows that he is George, but believes that his therapist, sitting in front of him, is an orphan. A closer look at this belief indicates that the patient has projected an aspect of his self representation onto the therapist. After a while George cries and states that it is he who feels like an orphan, unloved and rejected by his mother.

Fusion–defusion and introjective–projective cycles also occur in the formation of the "normal" seed of self. In fact, such relatedness, based perhaps on the representative biological functions of eating and spitting out food (Fenichel, 1945), are essential steps for normal psychic development. These ego functions serve to gather identifications, to enlarge the core of the self, promote its evolution, and establish more mature ego functions that are associated with the evolving core. The evolution of the self and the development and maturation of new ego functions reciprocally influence each other (Volkan, 1981). Gradually, the intensity and quickness of the primitive cycles give way to adaptive identifications that take place in more silent forms. In the presence of pathology, primitive ego mechanisms associated with the core are doomed to be repeated, as if there are continuous attempts to promote psychological growth within the core without success.

Affects

The nature of the affect that saturates the core of the self is the primary determinant of whether it will evolve or remain as a psychotic seed. If the mother–child interaction provides and supports "good" affects, and the components are also saturated with "good" affects, the core will have adequate nourishment to be "normal," to grow, and subsequently to manage "bad" affects without becoming fixated. Normally, "good" and "bad" affects contaminating the core will be tamed and integrated, giving the child a more realistic and integrated sense of self. Similarly, the child will have a more realistic sense of object representations when his or her affects pertaining to them are tamed and integrated. The seed will not evolve "normally" if saturated with "bad" affects.

Infants, however, are unable to name their affects; adults recognize the "good" ones as love, affection, and security, and the "bad" ones as rage, envy, and terror. Since the seed of madness is associated with "bad" affects, we can assume that anyone who becomes "mad," for example, schizophrenic, has a core structure that is saturated with horrible affects constituting a condition that can be called *infantile depression*.

Infantile depression is unlike typical adult depression, which is caused by object loss and followed by disruptive total identification with the representation of the lost object. With the depressed adult, aggression and libido originally directed toward the lost object engage in an ambivalent struggle. The internal world of the prototypically depressed adult becomes a battleground since both drive derivatives are attached to the hypercathected internalized object representation of the lost object with which the sufferer identifies. Infantile depression, however, arises from saturation of the infant's undifferentiated (or poorly differentiated) core self representation with "bad" (aggressively determined) affects that constantly assault the foundation and the building blocks of self. Thought disorders of patients with schizophrenia are secondary to the primary disturbance in taming "bad" affects.

In intensive psychoanalytically oriented treatment of individuals with schizophrenia, I have seen that structural change within the infantile psychotic self is not possible until the patient has reexperienced horrible affects and mastered the infantile depression. To arrive at this point, the therapist–patient relationship must gradually come to resemble a "good" and sustaining one between mother and child. This is why the therapist's use of countertransference is crucial (see chapter 7 by L. Bryce Boyer).

Infantile Psychotic Self

After intensive work for over thirty years with severely regressed or underdeveloped patients, including individuals with schizophrenia, it is my conclusion that no one becomes truly "mad" (i.e., schizophrenic) simply because of massive regression. Prototypical adult schizophrenia occurs in individuals who carry a psychotic "seed," which I call the *infantile psychotic self* (Volkan, 1994a, 1995). Before the crystallization of adult prototypical schizophrenia, the infantile psychotic self is enveloped by a healthier self. Adult schizophrenia is initiated when the encapsulated "mad" core can no longer be effectively controlled by those ego mechanisms associated with the healthier self and the individual (re)experiences infantile depression. In crystallized adult schizophrenia, the healthier self is replaced by a new, more primitive self associated with more primitive ego mechanisms. The adult with schizophrenia is regressed because of this replacement and because of the increased influence of the psychotic seed on the weaker "new" self. However, because every adult with schizophrenia retains aspects of the healthier self (Katan, 1954; Bion, 1957) the replacement falls short of being absolute.

The infantile psychotic self, the "seed of madness," is formed during the early interaction of mother and child or during marked regression *in the developmental years* in which the child's self representation is still flexible, and can be saturated with "bad" affects. For example, an unbearable trauma occurring in the developmental years, such as incest or the loss of a major object for which there is no substitute, can cause severe regression, shatter the self representation, and allow "bad" affects to flow into it and make it a psychotic seed. I do not believe that severe regression occurring after adolescence and the second individuation (Blos, 1979) can produce an infantile psychotic self. Severe regression in a situation as traumatic as the Holocaust can bring massive defensive regressive fixations to an adult; but, in my limited experience with this kind of trauma (Volkan, 1993), I have observed no creation of an infantile psychotic self.

Different Levels

The "seed of madness" differs from one patient to another although they are all alike in respect to the utilization by the associated primitive ego mechanisms of fusion-defusion, introjective–projective cycles, and the (re)activation of transitional objects and phenomena to relate to and control object relations. The infantile psychotic self can, however, be roughly classified according to hierarchical levels. In some, fusion-defusion dominates over introjective–projective relatedness. In this case, the infantile psychotic self is more primitive. Kernberg (1992) and D. Rosenfeld (1992) concur here, using slightly different terminology.

To elaborate, Kernberg sees dismantling of internalized object relations at the lowest level of the hierarchy, observing in slightly less severe conditions "The autistic encapsulation of early object relations under conditions of extreme trauma" (p. ix). He continues that in the middle range of severity, "we find the dominance of symbiotic, fused, or undifferentiated relations between self and object" (p. ix). Kernberg holds that differentiation occurs at the top of the hierarchy, and more sophisticated splits are played out in association with improved reality testing.

Furthermore, what the infantile psychotic self absorbs in the way of object images differs from individual to individual. Although it does not absorb growth-producing stable identifications, it does absorb some identifications with "part objects" (or remains in close fusion-defusion or introjective–projective relatedness with them). The nature of absorbed or closely related part objects makes one infantile psychotic self different from the other one. As the child grows, the individual's healthier aspect determines the way the seed of madness is perceived, controlled (absorbed and enveloped), and defined.

The Fates of the Infantile Psychotic Self

It is my belief that every adult who becomes schizophrenic has always had an infantile psychotic self, one originally formed or regressively appearing during the developmental years; but, the reverse is not true since the formation of a "seed of madness" does not necessarily lead to prototypical adult schizophrenia. There are several fates of the infantile psychotic self (Volkan, 1995):

1. An infantile psychotic self may shrink and disappear as the child has another chance to evolve a seed that is libidinally dominated. An analogy would be a tubercular lesion in a child's lungs that becomes calcified and "dead" forever. Unlike the calcified lesion, however, an inactive infantile psychotic self will not reveal itself on an X ray. Instead, it must be inferred when treatment succeeds in modifying and strengthening the self representation of the adult with schizophrenia without structurally changing the psychotic seed. For more than thirty years, I followed the course of such a patient, who exhibited no psychotic behavior following his treatment, and so concluded that his psychotic seed had become "calcified" (Volkan, 1995). Yet, I would not quarrel with anyone who sees the first disposition of the infantile psychotic self as only a theoretical possibility.

2. The second possibility is the opposite of the first: The childhood psychotic seed may persist into adult life, actively dominating the rest of the personality organization. This reduces the likelihood of any mature development of the individual's self representation, object relations, and ego

functions. He or she will exhibit childhood schizophrenia or retarded mental development or another primitive mental state, according to what it is called phenomenologically.

The last three outcomes pertain to "encapsulation" (H. Rosenfeld, 1965; Volkan, 1976, 1995; D. Rosenfeld, 1992) of the infantile psychotic self by the healthier self representation that evolved alongside the psychotic seed:

3. This possibility reflects only *partial* encapsulation of the infantile psychotic self and its considerable absorption from the developmental or adolescence years by the healthier self representation, which is then influenced by it and becomes its "voice." When this happens, the individual exhibits a *psychotic personality organization* as an adult. Ego mechanisms associated with the healthier self deal with this influence of the "seed of madness" in various ways. They might try to split off the partially encapsulated infantile psychotic self. However, this is not a stable and effective process since the infantile psychotic self has been largely assimilated by the healthier one; using ego mechanisms associated with the healthier self in *reenactments* maintains a sense of reality. These reenactments are repetitive, involuntary actions that promote an illusion of a fit between external reality and the infantile psychotic self, or the illusion of being able to start all over and to develop a core which is saturated with "good" (libidinal) affects (see chapter 5 by Volkan and Ast).

Persons with psychotic personality organization may seem normal at one level of functioning, but they have secret lives dominated by fusion-defusion and/or introjective–projective cycles which include paranoid fears or extreme idealizations, sexual or aggressive perversions, and psychosomatic expressions. For example, one patient who was a respected person in his professional life was engaged in pedophilic activities in order to create a "new" mother–child experience that might solidify a "new" and libidinally saturated infantile core. He failed miserably in these attempts, and was doomed to repeat his actions (Volkan, 1995).

4. The fourth possibility involves the eruption of a formerly encapsulated infantile psychotic self through a "crack" in the healthier self representation—without causing a generalized psychotic condition such as adult schizophrenia—but causing focalized bizarre behavior which may be transient or recurring in the absence of treatment.

5. The fifth outcome is associated with the development of adult prototypical schizophrenia—an adult becoming "mad." This reflects paralysis of ego mechanisms relating to the individual's healthier self (Pao, 1979), loss of identity, terror, and (re)experiencing infantile depression. Although a new self and identity to deal with the infantile psychotic core is quickly developed, it is no longer a "healthy" one; it gets directly linked to the psychotic seed, and absorbs it. The person who develops a psychotic personality organization absorbs the infantile psychotic self slowly while maintaining a sense of reality. Yet, in adult prototypical schizophrenia, such absorption is quick and without a sense of reality. Since this process is never completed, however, part of the personality remains uncontaminated. Ego mechanisms associated with the newly established and "sicker" self, *the adult psychotic self* (Volkan, 1994a,b, 1995) use primitive means, including delusions, hallucinations, language peculiarities, and bizarre reactivation of transitional objects and phenomena while acting as the "voice" of the "mad seed."

Biology and Psychology

Consideration of the infantile psychotic self suggests a new discussion of the way biological and psychological factors combine in the etiology of schizophrenia and related disorders. Currently, there are no unified biological theories explaining why madness occurs.

Among the sophisticated genetic researchers, Pekka Tieneri and his coworkers suggest that it is futile to attempt assessing the respective importance of genetic (biological) vulnerability and family environment (Tienari, 1991; Tienari, Sorri, Lahti, Naarala, Wahlberg, Ronkko, Pohjola, and Moring, 1985). Cancro (1986) declared that biological theories are in this connection "devoid of psychological content" and "increasingly suffer from reductionism" (p. 106), and a review of the biological research on schizophrenia supports Cancro's conclusions (Volkan, 1995). As technology progresses and increasing attention is paid to biological psychiatry, researchers continue to explore all of the possible aspects of schizophrenia. However, like the folk tale, it is as though many blind men were touching different parts of an elephant while failing to describe the animal as a whole. Although each investigator seems sure of his or her findings, there is not enough agreement at this time to yield definitive conclusions.

Along with Freud (1914) and Mahler (1968), I hold that both nature and nurture are involved in the etiology of schizophrenia and the formation of a psychotic seed. Yet as an analyst, I am more concerned about how the combination of biology and psychology create this condition together; affects, thoughts, and behavior are not easy to study. I have written elsewhere:

> At present we can speak of the nature–nurture issue in rather general terms: If a child has a biological weakness disturbing the ego functions that organize and integrate experiences, develop self- and object representations, form memories, maintain thoughts, tame unbearable and unnamable affects, and represses unacceptable conflicts, he may be prone to schizophrenia. . . . How a child, with a given biological state, experiences interaction with the environment, and how he assimilates such experiences into his developing mind, determines the juncture at which disposition and environmental influences meet [Volkan 1995, p. 67].

Biological and constitutional factors interfere with or enhance the child's ability to introject and identify with the functions of others; however, the child has no choice but to take in experiences from the environment. In the long run, the "mixing" of the components passing through the channel of the mother–child experiences sets up the foundations of the child's psychological structure.

Tähkä (1984, 1993) speaks of the infant's species-specific mental function potentials that develop into more sophisticated mental phenomena once they are activated. He divides them into two groups, the *fundamental* and the *complicated*. Perception and memory belong in the first; their activation is almost certain to occur in an average environment, such as nursing at the mother's breast.

More complicated relationships with others, for example with the mother, activate the advanced mental function potentials, according to Tähkä, and are then more vulnerable to deficiencies and complications in the interaction with the mother. Psychological determinants, such as identifications or responses to trauma, most likely are more dominant in the evolution of the seed of the self and its psychotic form when we consider the complicated mental function potentials.

I believe that if there is a genetic–biological disturbance influencing the infant's fundamental mental function potentials, the initial seed of self is laid down without much psychological content, and the resulting infantile psychotic self becomes more biologically determined than psychologically determined (Volkan, 1995). Childhood schizophrenia may result since biological determinants might not allow the evolution of a healthier self representation. Again, this is a difficult area to study since biology and psychology are barely differentiated at this level.

No doubt further research into infancy will identify and tell us more about both types of mental function potentials. This volume will explore the puzzling area of mind–body juncture and the components passing through the channel that cannot be measured by "scientific" research but which belong in the realm of psychology that deals with the dynamic unconscious.

We sometimes see severely disturbed individuals who are able to describe their inner worlds in uncanny ways. An example of a patient with a psychotic personality organization, is one who was in treatment with Dr. Gabriele Ast for over one year. This patient (discussed in chapter 5) was able to demonstrate her partially encapsulated infantile psychotic self, showing us the clinical expressions of the "seed of madness."

References

Apprey, M. (1993), Dreams of urgent–voluntary errands and transgenerational haunting and transsexualism. In: *Intersubjectivity, Projective Identification and Otherness*, ed. M. Apprey & H. F. Stein. Pittsburgh, PA: Duquesne University Press, pp. 102–128.

Bion, W. R. (1957), Differentiation of the psychotic from the non-psychotic personalities. *Internat. J. Psycho-Anal.*, 38:266–275.

Blos, P. (1979), *The Adolescent Passage*. New York: International Universities Press.

Cancro, R. (1986), General considerations relating to theory in the schizophrenic disorders. In: *Towards a Comprehensive Model for Schizophrenic Disorders*, ed. D. B. Finesilver. New York: Analytic Press, pp. 97–107.

Emde, R. (1988a), Development terminable and interminable. I. Innate and motivational factors from infancy. *Internat. J. Psycho-Anal.*, 69:23–41.

——— (1988b), Development terminable and interminable. II. Recent psychoanalytic theory and therapeutic considerations. *Internat. J. Psycho-Anal.*, 69:283-296.

Fenichel, O. (1945), *The Psychoanalytic Theory of Neuroses*. New York: W. W. Norton.

Freud, S. (1914), On the history of the psycho-analytic movement. *Standard Edition*, 14:1–66. London: Hogarth Press, 1957.

Greenspan, S. I. (1989), *The Development of the Ego: Implications for Personality Theory, Psychopathology and The Psychotherapeutic Process*. Madison, CT: International Universities Press.

Katan, M. (1954), The importance of the non-psychotic-part of the personality in schizophrenia. *Internat. J. Psycho-Anal.*, 35:119–128.

Kernberg, O. F. (1992), Foreword. In: *The Psychotic Aspects of the Personality* by D. Rosenfeld. London: Karnac Books, pp. vii–xiii.

Mahler, M. S. (1968), *On Human Symbiosis and the Vicissitudes of Individuation*. New York: International Universities Press.

Pao, P.-N. (1979), *Schizophrenic Disorders*. New York: International Universities Press.

Rosenfeld, D. (1992), *The Psychotic Aspects of the Personality*. London: Karnac Books.

Rosenfeld, H. A. (1965), *Psychotic States: A Psychoanalytic Approach*. London: Hogarth Press.

Spitz, R. A. (1957), *No and Yes: On the Beginning of Human Communication*. New York: International Universities Press.

———— (1965), *The First Year of Life*. New York: International Universities Press.

Tähkä, V. (1984), Psychoanalytic treatment as a developmental continuum: Consideration on disturbed structuralization and its phase-specific encounter. *Scand. Psychoanal. Rev.*, 7:133–159.

———— (1993), *Mind and Its Treatment: A Psychoanalytic Approach*. Madison, CT: International Universities Press.

Tienari, P. (1991), Interaction between genetic vulnerability and family environment: The Finnish adoptive family study of schizophrenia. *Acta Psychiatr. Scand.*, 84:460–465.

Tienari, P., Sorri, A., Lahti, I., Naarala, M., Wahlberg, K.-E., Ronkko, T., Pohjola, J., & Moring, J. (1985), The Finnish adoptive family study of schizophrenia. *Yale J. Biol. & Med.*, 58:227–237.

Volkan, V. D. (1976), *Primitive Internalized Object Relations: A Clinical Study of Schizophrenic, Borderline, and Narcissistic Patients*. New York: International Universities Press.

———— (1981), Transference and countertransference: An examination from the point of view of internalized object relations. In: *Object and Self: A Developmental Approach*, ed. S. Tutman, C. Kaye, & M. Zimmerman. New York: International Universities Press, pp. 429–451.

———— (1993), What the Holocaust means to a non-Jewish psychoanalyst. In: *Persistent Shadows of the Holocaust: The Meaning To Those Not Directly Affected*, ed. R. Moses. Madison, CT: International Universities Press, pp. 81–117.

———— (1994a), Psychodynamic formulations for psychotherapy of schizophrenic patients. *Directions in Psychiatry* (Special Report), Vol. 14.

———— (1994b), Identification with the therapist functions and ego-building in the treatment of schizophrenia. *Brit. J. Psychiatry* (Suppl.), 23:77–82.

———— (1995), *The Infantile Psychotic Self and Its Fates: Understanding and Treating Schizophrenics and Other Difficult Patients*. Northvale, NJ: Jason Aronson.

Part Two

Theory,
Clinical Illustrations,
and
Techniques

2

On the Origins of the Body Ego and Its Implications for Psychotic Vulnerability

JOHANNES LEHTONEN, M.D.

In the "Outline" Freud wrote (1940, p. 144) that the biological and psychological facts of mental life are like two end points of our knowing. We can say nothing about the relation between them except, perhaps in the future to describe the localization in the brain of mental events, without this helping us, however, anywhere in understanding them. In *The Ego and the Id* (1923) he defined the ego first and foremost as a body ego, a psychical projection or outcome of body surface experiences in the earliest phases of life. He did not describe the nature of the body ego in detail, however.

Although fundamental to the structural view, the clinical manifestations of the body ego in adults are still not very well

Acknowledgment: Support from the Signe and Ane Gyllenberg Foundation is gratefully acknowledged.

19

known. Freud's view of the body ego as the source of all later ego development, implied a real contact between the bodily and mental phenomena in the developing human being. After his preliminary formulation, the concept of the body ego has nevertheless received relatively little attention and the nature of the contact continues to be enigmatic. We agree only in general terms, that the basic layers of the personality are born out of the early interplay between the infant and the mother. We agree further, that the vital satisfactions the mother gives to the infant are crucial for early development, but our ideas about how the primordial ego, the body ego,[1] is formed out of these satisfactions are spread amongst many different kinds of theories and unintegrated clinical and empirical observations.

Fusion between the Infant and the Mother

In spite of the fact, that for a priori reasons we cannot fully understand how biological events may turn into, or at least influence mental phenomena, we are on firm ground when we say that the little newborn baby might know something more about it, since his or her vital task in the beginning of life is to find a way to a satisfactory overall mental state amongst the turbulent early happenings encountered at and immediately after the birth.

In a basic and simple sense the early psychophysical satisfactions brought about by sucking and other nourishment yield for the newborn simultaneously an affective satisfaction and provide it with life-giving events. There arises during early nursing a selfobject fusion between the infant and the mother, and simultaneously there occurs within the infant a fusion between affective experience of a vital satisfaction with sense

---

[1]I will hold predominantly to the concept of the body ego instead of the body self in order to underline the natural link existing between Freud's formulations and the primordial developmental events of early infancy, although clinically the body self might be a better concept in many instances.

impressions and perceptions pertinent to the situation. The ensuing satisfactions endow the infant's perceptual experiences (in the mouth, mucosa, skin, and gradually also hearing and sight) with a cathexis of tension relief, that is, with a primal pleasurable affect (Spitz, 1955).

My aim in this paper (Lehtonen [1991] was a preliminary communication) is to suggest that the vital processes connected with a fusion of infant and mother, taking place first and foremost in breast-feeding, form the nuclear events which precipitate the birth and development of the body ego. In this paper, I will clarify in more detail what I mean by the term *body ego*. That primal psychological structure to which different authors assign different names, such as Spitz's (1955) primal cavity, Weil's (1970) basic core, Pacella's (1980) primal matrix, can be equated with my term *body ego* following Freud's (1923) original aphoristic delineation: the body ego as psychic projection of the body surface.

When the experiences of satisfaction fuse with perceptual and other somatic processes that are integral to primal satisfaction, the nucleus of the ego experience shifts beyond the sphere of immediate perceptual events. There emerge in the infant new psychical qualities, which form a basis for a new, previously nonexistent level of experience. In this process, the original transient perceptual events, stemming from outside sources, are changed gradually into a more lasting and satisfying state in the infant's mind. Charged with a feeling of satisfaction, the singular impressions are immersed in one diffuse, satisfying experience. Rene Spitz (1957) characterizes this process as leading to a coenesthetic organization of the psyche in which perception still takes place in totality and not yet in a diacritic, differentiated way. The somatic and psychic components of the experience cannot yet be differentiated. Instead they fuse with each other, and as a result, the primordial ego nucleus (body ego), when born, is inherently "bilingual," speaking the two tongues of somatic biology and the primitive psychology of oral instinctual satisfactions.

Easson (1973), Hoffer (1981), and Glenn (1993) have also emphasized the new psychological organization emerging from the primal satisfactions.

The Changes Brought about by the Birth Process

Elementary perceptions occur at the fetal stage through auditory experiences, rocking movements, and casual thumbsucking (Piontelli, 1988, 1989; Vauhkonen, 1990). The birth of the child, its emergence from the intrauterine environment into a genuine relationship with the mother and the rest of the outside world, brings about a crucial change in the infant's psychophysical balance. Instead of the continuous energy supply from the mother's circulation, the infant has to start to breathe on her own. The intrauterine transfusion is substituted by feeding from a new, previously unknown, and less predictable source, the external mother and her breast.

The changes brought about by birth make the infant totally dependent on an object relationship and on the previously unknown external world. This leads to unavoidable experiences of loss of satisfaction and loss of the object. In comparison to the fetal world, the peri- and postnatal experiences are of an unprecedented nature for the infant, and entirely new factors become conditions of not only physical, but also psychological survival (Greenacre, 1952). The emergence and preservation of the postnatal states of satisfaction, out of which the primary identification (Hoffer, 1981), a kind of protoimage of the self of the infant is formed, will thereafter rest on the intense and vitally satisfying fusional experiences at the mother's breast and the other care comparable to it. The primary satisfactions also have a special intensity due to their vital nature. They change the bodily state of the infant and simultaneously lead to affective pleasurable satisfaction and tension relief. Spitz (1957, p. 78) describes the outcome as archaic preimagery material.

However, on account of the possibility of a loss of satisfaction as part of the natural course of infant care, these early events leave traces in the newborn, which are more profound than any other sense impressions not connected with similar vital meaning. The early satisfactions, together with their counterpart, the experience of absence of satisfaction, gradually call for the development of reality testing; that is, finding out whether the object is there or not, as underlined by Spitz (1957, p. 21).

The self experience born out of these events is in an obvious way primarily unconscious and remains so, for the body ego at this level cannot yet be connected with verbal communication. Once born, however, the primary layer of the psyche can later be approached verbally, when it has been activated in a communicative relationship, by physical or sexual pleasure, and also by musical and other artistic experiences, and brought to a level where it can be communicated. Or it can appear in pathological forms, as in primitive modes of transference and in certain types of hypnagogic manifestations, as will be described later.

The Point of View of the Cathexis

Being anchored to the unconscious, the body ego is a difficult object for study. The organizing viewpoints of my approach are the role of the fusion between perceptual experiences and affects, and the selfobject fusion, which take place in the very first interactions between infant and mother and have a cathecting influence on the nascent self of the infant.

The extensive literature (Greenacre, 1952; Spitz, 1955, 1957, 1959; Spitz, Emde and Metcalf, 1970; Mahler, Pine, and Bergman, 1975; Stern, 1985; Greenspan, 1992) on the early development of the infant and the infant–mother interplay, predominantly apply other standpoints than mine. I want to underline that in an obvious way the body ego development is enmeshed with the complexity of many significant developmental events and phenomena. The different points of view relevant for understanding the emergence of the personality in the beginning of life are multiple and do not exclude each other. Direct comparison between the work of different authors is not easy because of the use of different terminology, concepts, and viewpoints.

It is clear that such developmental processes take place before any kind of object constancy can prevail in the infant's mind. At this stage the infant's self and object experiences fuse together. Neither the self nor the object can be identified as separate entities, just as hydrogen and oxygen cannot be separately distinguished in water. Gradually, when the infant has enjoyed a sufficient amount of satisfying fusion with the mother, the nucleus of the body ego, which entails emergent self aspects, begins to consolidate. This prepares the infant for a symbiotic kind of object relationship, but the development of object constancy still lies long ahead (Mahler et al., 1975).

I will return later to the relation between the body ego and the body image, but I want to point out that the body image, because of its connections to conscious and preconscious psychical qualities, is a later and more developed phenomenon than the body ego. It unfolds gradually from the body ego as a function of the infant–mother relationship when the infant's needs and overall psychophysiological state are recognized, adequately met, and communicated in the interplay between infant and mother (Scott, 1948; Winnicott, 1971; Hagglund and Piha, 1980). The body image development requires more articulated and increasingly verbalizable interactions between infant and mother than the body ego, which is primarily connected to the vital satisfactions, tension relief, sleep, and basic welfare; that is, the world of deepest security according to Spitz (1955) or to the ego security positioning according to Pacella (1980).

The Isakower Phenomenon

At first sight it may look unlikely, that any kind of clinical evidence could be gleaned which would lend credible support to the relation of very early developmental events to a metapsychological concept of the body ego. This is so especially with regard to clinical work with adults, whereas the psychology of children is in a natural way richer in body ego issues (Hoffer, 1981; Furman, 1992).

Two phenomena derived from clinical psychoanalytic experience, related by their discoverers several decades ago to the infant's early experiences of sucking at the breast, may throw light on the psychological consequences of the psychophysical selfobject fusion experienced by the infant at the breast. In 1938, Otto Isakower described a hypnagogic phenomenon he had observed in several patients. When falling asleep, and under certain other conditions, a child and occasionally also an adult may have the sensation, as a hypnagogic visual experience, of an undefined or round surface or a grayish mass, which approaches closer, grows bigger, and may be crumpled or creased. The experience is often accompanied by sensations in the mouth. As the image recedes, it diminishes and disappears. It does not have at any stage a distinct, recognizable shape or color as a physical object and it is therefore not a genuine hallucination.

Isakower suggested that the phenomenon represents a perceptual memory of an infant's experience at the mother's breast, a large soft mass, a surface difficult to perceive distinctly from the infant's point of view. It approached, filled the mouth, and again receded, diminished, and disappeared. The unclear perceptual character is typical of the experience and suggests that it is a result of the melting together of more than one kind of influence.

Various *derivatives* of the Isakower phenomenon are not unfrequent in analytical practice, depending greatly on how they are defined, but distinctly similar phenomena as described by him are not common. When recognized, the Isakower phenomenonevokes natural curiosity. Considering its early and developmentally significant nature, it is somewhat surprising that the phenomenology has not received more attention and the relevant literature is relatively sparse, especially during recent years (Kepecs, 1952; Heilbrunn, 1953; Garma, 1955, 1974; Sperling, 1957; Easson, 1973; Richards, 1985; Dann, 1992; Glenn, 1993). A vignette given to me by the supervisor of the therapist treating Ms. A, 15 years old, demonstrates some qualities of the Isakower phenomenon.

Ms. A was referred to a child psychiatric treatment and further to psychotherapy after having started to lose weight at the age of 15. She had frequent stomach upsets and vomiting in childhood and remembered her mother being angry with her on those occasions. She usually received special attention when ill and she was taken to the parents' bed or they came to comfort her when she had grown too big to get in bed with them.

At kindergarten age she had frequent nightmares which she remembered and told to her therapist in the opening phase. But she did not return to them nor did she report any other dreams during the following year in the therapy. The nightmares repeated the same situation and feeling: she was between two large and crushing figures and she was unable to breathe and felt as if she were being squeezed.

The nightmares were probably related to her experiences with her parents in bed and seemed to be oedipally charged images, but there may have been a deeper meaning relating to her early experiences at her mother's breasts, which the two vague and large, but crushing figures may have resembled.

Isakower interpreted the hypnagogic manifestations as a regressive, defensive retreat from threatening incestuous impulses activated by masturbation. Kepecs (1952), Heilbrunn (1953), Fink (1967), Richards (1985), and Dann (1992) have presented clinical data supporting this view. Sperling (1957) has stressed the role of ego mastery in using the Isakower phenomenon and oral satisfactions like thumb-sucking as a regressive retreat from more demanding developmental scenes.

In a penetrating study of the phenomenon and its roots in the earliest formative stages of ego development, William Easson (1973) has taken the standpoint that "it should be possible to use the relatively easily recognized Isakower complex of memories as a way to investigate the earliest ego state" (p. 66), and that "in the development of the very primitive ego during earliest infancy, it can be postulated that there first exists in the experiencing mind, mere floating, turning, whirling sensations, sensations of *being* in some fashion. These may represent the initial inner awareness of physical existence." A similar idea is expressed by Hoffer (1981). Spitz (1955) builds his conceptualization of the role of the primal oral cavity as the origin of perception and the primal psychological organization of the infant, explicitly on Isakower's work. Easson, though he acknowledges that the Isakower phenomenon may be remembered with memories superimposed from later developmental stages, and can function in this fashion as a regressive defense against disturbing recollections, remarks (p. 61) that the later superimposed meanings of the complex may tend to obscure the more significant and basic importance of Isakower-type memories.

Dreaming, the Dream Screen,
and the Nascent Ego

A few years later, based in part on Isakower's description, Bertram Lewin (1946, 1948, 1953) reported another phenomenon, which he named the "dream screen." One of his patients, while recollecting her dream during the analytic hour, experienced that the dream contents were at a remove from her, as they would have been displayed on a screen, which was rolled up. From this and some other clinical vignettes Lewin concluded, that underlying ordinary dream images there is a blank empty dream matrix comparable to a film projection screen, which represents the primordial dream and upon which the ordinary dream images are imposed. Lewin suggested that the primordial dream screen represents the fulfillment of the primary wish to sleep and the desire for rest. Typical dreams which are able to realize this wish and which may lack content, are the wet dreams of young adolescents leading to an orgasmic release. Lewin referred to them as "blank dreams." Rycroft (1951), Kanzer (1954), Boyer (1960), and Garma (1974) have confirmed his basic observations.

The original ego ensuing from the events delineated is a pure pleasure ego, while it is the outcome of a vital satisfaction. Lewin (1946, 1948) pointed out that after the infant's experience of satisfaction at sucking he or she typically falls asleep and achieves in this way the fulfillment of its most fundamental desire, satiation of hunger and achievement of rest devoid of any disturbing excitements. Lewin did not, however, attribute any role to the ego in this process.

The dream screen as an internalized transformation of the original perceptual experiences arising in breast-feeding may well represent the fulfillment of the primary wishes. A concept like this is closely related to Freud's view of the origin of psychosexuality. He regarded the infant's experience at the mother's breasts and the satiated falling asleep following it as the prime form of psychosexual satisfaction and a model also for the pattern of adult sexual satisfaction.

Thus it looks as if the difficult and fundamental question of how energy with psychic qualities can emerge from biological processes (Pacella, 1980), may gain more meaning, when the primordial significance of the oral satisfactions arising from breast-feeding and other surrogate satisfactions are considered. The satisfactions lead gradually to the formation of the pleasure-maintaining body ego, with the blank state as its primary form. A similar fusion, as in oral experiences, takes place also in adult genital intercourse, which involves fusion between affect and physical experience as well as between self and object. Also another trait common to an oral and genital satisfaction exists, namely the achievement of complete fulfillment of the instinctual needs. So, the phenomena in question are not restricted to the early developmental stages alone, but can also be recognized as elements in the primal psychology of adults.

Although Spitz disagreed with Lewin about the visual nature of the Isakower phenomenon and suggested the mother's face and not the breast as its source, he agreed with Lewin about the significance of the primal oral satisfactions as the origin of archaic psychological experience. He wrote (Spitz, 1957, p. 77) that the relief of unpleasant tension (through oral satisfactions) may have functioned as the most archaic matrix for the dream screen. He added that therefore, the dream screen of the adult appears to be a representation of the most archaic human pleasure experience.

Willi Hoffer's (1981) work is also highly illuminating about the relation of the dream screen and the earliest psychological experiences. Oral eroticism, skin sensitivity, hypnagogia, and the psychology of dreaming are connected. He acknowledges the difficulty in understanding these early phenomena due to the lack of ordinary ego and superego functions, and states that it is a question of a no-man's-land between biology and psychology. He is unambiguous, however, in equating the early satisfactions with primary identification which, compared to more developed psychological functions, still lacks cognitive discrimination and consists of pure feeling awareness. The works of Heilbrunn (1953), Kanzer (1954), Easson (1973), and Gammill (1980) on the dream screen agree with this.

The activation of the dream screen in adult transference, the starting point of the original work by Lewin, has been elaborated further by Rycroft (1951), and by Boyer (1960) in a detailed study of two patients. According to both, the dream screen is able to support a double cathexis, a narcissistic one and an object related real person cathexis, which makes the dream screen into a bridge from a narcissistic orientation to object relations. Their view is perfectly in line with Spitz's (1957, p. 80) understanding of the meaning of the oral intake of the breast for the infant as a matrix for object relations.

The Boundaries of the Body Ego

The boundaries of the body ego are not primarily related to physical space, but to the intensity and duration of the pleasure arising out of the satisfactions. Our boundary conception is closely related with our physical space conception and it is essential to stress the metaphoric character of the boundary concept relevant to the nascent body ego (see also Lewin, 1953, p. 176; Scott, 1985). The true limits of the body ego are not based on the physical boundaries of the body, but on the durability and strength of the psychic satisfaction. The boundaries of the primitive body ego coincide with the primal affect of satisfaction. The existence of the satisfactory body ego state ceases together with the waning of the satisfying affect, when the infant is left long enough without further supply from the mother.

The experience of the continuity of the body ego is therefore fragile early on. It can easily be threatened by various factors, especially instinctual tensions like hunger. Also external factors like traumatic experiences and overwhelming stimuli can have the same effect (Garma, 1974).

When perceptual events become connected with satisfaction, they are transformed by the cathecting effects into a new object and pleasure related mode, and the nascent body ego will develop a shield against direct stimuli by means of a barrier (Kepecs, 1952; Spitz, 1955; Gediman, 1971), whose protective power depends, aside from innate factors, first and foremost on the strength of pleasure arising in the satisfactory fusion. A similar kind of interpretation of the role of the dream screen, an equivalent of the body ego, has been given by Abse (1977). According to him, the satisfaction-yielding psychic experiences are translated by means of the dream screen from the perceptual to the conceptual sphere, from phenomenon to noumenon.

The transformation in question may shed some light also on the genetic origin of the principle, that the unconscious mind can be approached only indirectly (Gammill, 1980). In order to approach the unknown and unobservable core of the mind (Enckell, 1988), it becomes necessary to look for the meanings which exist behind any observable data. The essence of the topographical principle may thus be traced back to the nascent processes of ego formation in the early fusional experiences, which by their very nature cannot be described directly by any means, only by means of their consequences. Spitz (1957) aims at the same level of experience in his notion of the coenesthetic organization. He suggests that the early differentiation of the mind to the topographical organization can begin only after consolidation of the primal, pure pleasure/affect organization. Only thereafter can the first object relations start to develop, heralded by the specific smiling response of the infant, in parallel to the unfolding of the reality testing function.

Freud put the relation between the id and the ego in a simple and clear way: The ego arises from the id when the id comes in contact with the outside world. The fusion of pleasure with the infant's perceptual experiences is merely another way of describing the same event. If we approach the id's contact with the external world from the point of view of fusion of perception and affect in breast-feeding and surrogate satisfactions, we may broaden our view of the origin of the basic psychoanalytic developmental concepts in relation to early infant–mother interplay and psychosomatic events connected with it, and bring more details to the picture of how the birth of the self-ego occurs in this process.

While there is a fusion of the self and object in the mouth–nipple and skin contact, the emergent body ego is derived in an essential way both from the mother and the infant. Their respective share in this process can be separated only artificially. This feature in the origin of the ego implies a primordial integration of the self and the object in the very beginning. Repercussions of this feature may be found in primary process thinking and dreaming. Traits belonging to the dreaming subject are often interchangeable with some aspects of the objects dreamed about (Lewin, 1955; Garma, 1974). The subject–object logic ceases and there may be a total interchangeability of self and object images in dreaming, in the same way that infant and mother cannot be distinguished in the early fusional experiences.

Physiological Aspects

Whilst we know that the infant's experiences of satisfaction are normally followed by sleep and dreaming, the infant's neurobiological responses to breast-feeding and other vital nursing have not yet been studied. It seems nevertheless plausible that the satisfying experiences of nursing impinge on the infant's mind close to the dream state and leave their traces in those physiological processes which participate in dream formation. The satisfying experiences probably charge the physiological dream processes with pleasure and make them in this way capable vehicles of psychological experiencing. The blank dream of a full and complete satisfaction as Lewin (1946) has described it, may represent the most elementary form of experience that may evolve intrapsychically from the primal satisfactions. A mechanism like this might be able to give psychological meaningfulness also to the structural similarity that is found between the physiology of dreaming and the psychological primary process of dreams (Lehtonen, 1980).

Morton Reiser's (1990) line of thought concerning neurobiological effects of affective experiences follows a similar argument. He has pointed out that affective experiences create connections in the neural pathways in the developing nervous system and contribute to the emergence of dreams which always have an affective experience as their nodal focus. The different threads of thoughts weaving together the dream converge in this "kernel" and disappear in it beyond the scope originally assumed by Freud (1900). This blank central point of the dream may represent the dream's affective core, and it can probably be traced back in its very origin to the real satisfactions of the infant during the early postnatal period of life.

The Nature of the Affects Related
to the Isakower Phenomenon

Isakower described the sensations of the hypnagogic experience predominantly in adults, that is, long after the original oral experiences and thus in a context of a relatively mature personality, which must be taken into account when interpreting his observations. The hypnagogic experience was described by his patients as a sense of a revolving disk, dizziness, or as a strange sense of familiarity similar to the déjà vu sensations occurring during the epileptic aura. Isakower's patients could also feel that the mouth was full and the whole body might be in a state of floating or sinking. Sometimes there was also the sense of the body becoming united or merged with the environment. Cutaneous sensations were frequent.

Generally speaking the feelings and sensations occurring were neither particularly pleasant nor unpleasant, but rather an undefined tension, with a sense of relief as the sensation disappeared. The experiences could be mediated through various senses, and the boundaries between the body and the external world seemed to disappear. In the visual field a shadowy circular object sometimes appeared, which approached, was felt to crush the person, and again receded into the distance. Auditory perception might yield sensations of humming and muttering. The mouth was felt to be filled with a mass which could be freely examined and even figures could be drawn on it. These sensations could be voluntarily maintained. In other words, the reality testing function was fully operational during these experiences.

Spitz (1955) describes the nature of the primal cavity, which he more or less equates with the Isakower phenomenon, in the following way:

> The world of the primal cavity is a strange one: indistinct, vague, pleasurable and unpleasurable at the same time. It bridges the chasm between inside and outside, between passivity and action. These experiences are dealt with on the level of the primal process, yet they lead to the development of the secondary process. It is a matrix for introjection and projection. The primal cavity is the cavernous home of the dreams [pp. 236–237].

According to Isakower, in the hypnagogic stage the cathexis of the object world weakens and the subject's own body cathexis increases. In this way the need to maintain the boundary between the body and the environment becomes less important. Lewin stressed the central role of the oral libido and satisfaction in the experiences connected with the dream screen. He regarded the wish represented by the dream screen as a pure form of the wish to sleep in peace. He did not attribute any role to the ego in this process. The sensory contents related to the dream screen experience may have a mechanical character of somewhat the same kind as that Isakower described in the hypnagogic state. Lewin's patients too reported having oral sensations in relation to the dream.

The body ego cannot be understood, however, solely in terms of the pleasure principle. The pure wish to sleep fulfills not only the desire for pleasure, but also the desire to be released from all tension. Lewin (1946, 1948) pointed out that in depression and suicide attempts there is a desire for a satisfaction comparable to the primordial sleep, a wish to gain a totally undisturbed rest, implying a close tie between pleasure and the deathwish. It thus seems that the genesis of the body ego involves not only a fusion of perception and satisfaction, the self and the object, but also a fusion of the basic drives (see also Spitz, 1957, p. 80).

Only when the infant starts differentiating from the first personal object and begins to become psychologically separate, will the infant gradually be endowed with a self with affect qualities bearing a reference to distinct personal object relations (Tähkä, 1993). The primary infant–mother relation derived from their fusion, is still characterized by a two-dimensional mode of functioning on a pleasure–unpleasure axis, and the affects have a different, more primitive nature than affects developing within object relations and capable of being communicated verbally.

The descriptive differentiation between vital versus categorical affects made by Stern (1985) seems relevant to the difference which can be made between affects characteristic to the body ego and to a more developed object oriented ego, respectively. An ego capable of experiencing true affects connected to other persons begins to develop during the separation process. When the infant becomes able to endure helplessness, emptiness, and the pain of separateness, a capacity for object related affects will begin to emerge (Mahler et al., 1975).

Clinical derivatives can be encountered, especially in schizoid or clinging and psychosomatically inclined patients, who sometimes have great difficulty in expressing themselves verbally and tend to create an anaclitic relation to their therapists (Boyer, 1960; McDougall, 1989). Thorhild Leira (1995) has given an illuminating report of three different patients, who remained silent for long times in therapy and who slowly changed their relationship toward the therapist and began to use symbolic expression, which enabled them to find their way out from the silence. Leira describes their change as a move from two-dimensional factual to three-dimensional affective-symbolic and verbal psychological functioning. The change she describes in her patients resembles closely the difference I want to make between the essentially nonverbal, sometimes strangely factual, flattened, and concrete body ego states versus the psychological states characteristic of the more developed affect and object related ego.

Michael, one of William Easson's (1973) patients, experienced vivid Isakower phenomena during the psychotherapy sessions. He described the general kind of feeling he had during his psychotherapy conversation as his way of "just being together," a similar state to that described by Leira. Michael could experience during the session a feeling of floating, whirling, and gently turning, a state which he found as a "fulfillment." Easson suggested that Michael may have been recalling very early sensations of what it was to exist before he was a separate, discrete "I"; how it felt before he had an ego nucleus on which to focus, to anchor, and to integrate his perception. However, the establishment of an integrated ego nucleus and the recognition of this established ego made it possible for him to remember or reexperience sensations before he had this psychic core. Easson explicitly connects such phenomena to the body ego (p. 69), which according to him may have developed out of such experiential foci.

Winnicott describes the early state of undifferentiation and the sense of complete rest and fulfillment in a beautiful, almost poetical way in his unpublished notes on "Early Stages: Primary Introduction to External Reality," quoted by Davis and Wallbridge (1981, p. 39):

> [I]n the quiet moments let us say that there is no line but just lots of things they separate out, sky seen through trees, something to do with mother's eyes all going in and out, wandering around. Some lack of need for any integration. . . . That is an extremely valuable thing to be able to retain. Miss something without it. Something to do with being calm, restful, relaxed and feeling one with people and things when no excitement is around.

There is a difference between Winnicott and Isakower, however, since in Winnicott's description perhaps the greatest bliss is related to awareness of the presence of mother's eyes, whereas in the Isakower phenomenon distinct external persons are not present. Interestingly, Garma (1974) gives clinical material suggesting that in the color blue there is a projection taking place between early experiences with the breast and perception of the environment, the sky, in a similar spirit to Winnicott's description.

A Clinical Vignette

The sometimes almost strangely physical and mechanical character of experience, lacking in ordinary affect and often connected with budding anxiety, was displayed in a dream told to me by a male patient in his forties, at the beginning of the final stretch of his four-and-a-half-year analysis. He had sought treatment because of panic attacks during which he was afraid of becoming paralyzed down one side of his body. He was also dissatisfied with his work and with what he saw as his professional future.

During the years of analytic work his attitude toward me changed very slowly and reluctantly from early mistrust, wardedness, unaffective expression, querulousness, and a demonstrated distortion of his own thought sequences. It gradually turned toward acceptance, libidinal feelings, growing appreciation of our joint work, and a wish to also use his analytic experience in his own work.

When resuming the analysis after the last summer break he told me of a dream in which he was engaged in some kind of a mechanical movement, perhaps sexual intercourse, which gave rise to an unpleasant mechanical feeling. Then something round, perhaps a ball, began to approach, and he was overcome by intense anxiety.

He did not make distinct associations to the dream nor display other obvious currently significant connections to it in his life. He told about it, as he often did of significant experiences, in a somewhat remote way. However, at those times during the last phase of his analysis, he had begun to think and feel much more warmly about his parents whom he had until then expressed bitterness toward throughout the analysis. Neglect had been the central issue. He repeatedly criticized his parents for not having cared about him and the other three children. Both of the parents were career-oriented professionals. Speaking of his mother, he said repeatedly that he had not had a mother. During the most extreme of his feelings he would turn and twist on the couch, cry with a strange broken voice, bang his fist against the wall, and whimper. During the last year of his treatment he had, however, slowly begun to accept his parents as they actually were and to be more moderate in his demands and accusations. Sometime after the hour when he related the above dream experience to me, he again visited his parents, who lived in another town. When he was driving back home he was overcome by a powerful sadness. He wept, and he felt able to accept and forgive his parents. At the same time his attitude toward me also began to change from suspiciousness and unwillingness to share our work toward full cooperation and acceptance of our relation.

His dream expressed his still existing anxiety about exclusion, general lack of feeling, and fear of separation, extending to the level of the body ego experience. The dream did not wake him up, however, so the frustrations were now tolerable on the whole in spite of their threatening character. The ball approaching in the dream was most likely a condensed symbol of phallic sexuality and an early breast mother toward whom he had passionate wishes and simultaneously intense fears of exclusion and loss of satisfaction of his wishes expressed by reversal in the approaching ball. The bare and primitive symbolic expression in the dream connects it to the sexual body ego level of self experience.

Repression and the Body Ego

Satisfactions ensuing from fusional experiences of the infant in breast-feeding and other vital care, maintain in the infant a blank state of primal psychophysiological satiety. The blank state of satisfied calmness, which often leads to falling asleep, seems to be able to function besides as the supportive structure of basic well-being, as a repressing force against new stimuli impinging upon the infant either from outside or inside. Clinging to the blank state of satisfaction implies a repression of anything that may threaten this basic body ego state. Repression at this primordial level of psychological functioning is most likely related to, if not identical with, what Freud (1915) described as primal repression. Freud assumed that the psychophysiological excitations arising in the body are repelled and prevented from entering consciousness. This he saw as a necessary precondition for true psychological experiences to arise.

It seems meaningful to interpret primal repression as the attempt of the nascent body ego to preserve its own continuity of existence and repel everything that might disturb it. Like overwhelming endogenic psychophysiological tensions and absence of satisfaction, which may both threaten the nascent ego with annihilation. Repressive aspects of the functions of the dream screen have been emphasized also by Kepecs (1952), Lewin (1953), and Kanzer (1954). Joyce McDougall (1989) has suggested that especially psychosomatic patients use primal repression in their intense efforts to destroy any budding emotions felt to be threatening. A link between primal repression and vital affects has been posed also by Salonen (1979), though from a different angle.

Primitive forms of repression are, however, encountered also in relatively healthy subjects, for instance when a collusion with the basic boundaries of psychological experiencing happens to take place for one or another reason. The following vignette may illustrate this.

Mr. F, who had been in psychoanalysis for a year, at the beginning of the session described his general mood as somewhat subdued. He reminded me—he had spoken of this before—

that he would miss next week's sessions due to a business trip to another city. He said, maybe with a slight aura of hypocrisy, that he felt helpless because he had to travel and be away. During the preceding session when talking of the same feeling, he had recalled how, when he was 3 years old, his parents spent several months in another town and he was taken care of by his grandparents.

The present mood, however, was not related to that, but to the break in the analysis. He then began thinking about the projects he was involved in and about their completion. It occurred to him that he would bring me the finished papers. He thought about how he would organize them, and specifically how his analyst would look in that situation. I asked for his thoughts about it and he said that I would be pleased and would say something simple like, "Well, there it is." He added that the situation was somewhat similar to when he used to bring his school report home for his parents. He watched how his father looked when he read his report card. He got ice cream as a reward for a good report. It tasted good. It had to be a real ice cream cone. Ice cream in a dish wouldn't have tasted nearly as good.

Then he was silent and I asked him what the ice cream reminded him of. He responded immediately: "Nothing at all." There was a pause, and he said: "When you asked me that, it stopped me. I got stuck, somehow in emptiness. My mind couldn't move forward or back." Then he was quiet again for a while, and said, "I had a strange idea. I was looking at those holes in the ceiling. (Soundproof tiles with small holes in them.) I would melt into those holes, those four holes up there. Actually I'm already there. Next time I come for analysis, I'll take myself out of there."

Though the episode was an innocent one in the sense that it was not charged with powerful anxiety, Mr. F's fantasy about his ice cream seemed to be a remote derivative from the primal satisfactions. His psychological economy circulated in many other respects around primal satisfactions, probably because he had been compelled to share his early development and motherly care with his twin sibling. When I questioned his fantasy of satisfaction, it caused his thoughts to come to a stop. He found himself for a moment in a state of nothingness out of which he escaped by means of a merger fantasy.

Another vignette from a brief moment in the analysis of Mrs. B, to be described more fully later, demonstrates further how pleasure and a repressive wish to turn away from objects can become intertwined and connected to the current transference feeling, which was disappointment also in this case.

> I had changed the time of Mrs. B's Friday hour. She forgot the changed time, however, and did not appear. The following night she dreamed that she had overslept her hour and reported this dream to me the next day. I replied that she had used the previous day's session during the night in order to obtain such a comforting dream. "That's true," was her brief response.

So it looks as if the primal pleasures arising out of satisfactions and the repressive attempts to maintain this state could be seen as two different aspects of the same phenomenon. Satisfaction maintains the primitive affect of pleasure, and repression is an attempt to ensure its preservation. Defensive aspects of the dream screen were analyzed by Lewin (1953). Kepecs (1952) and Kanzer (1954) have also contributed ideas on this issue.

A somewhat related view has been presented by Joyce McDougall (1989). She has suggested that psychosomatic patients direct intense destructive efforts against any budding primitive emotions, a phenomenon related by her to primal repression. Salonen (1979) has posed a link between primal repression and vital affects, though from a different angle, by underlining the necessity for normal functioning of primal repression in order for vital affects to be experienced at all.

*The Relation between the Body Ego
and the Body Image*

The concept of the body ego and its founding role in general ego development stems from Freud's (1923) outline of structural theory. The concept of the body image was described by Paul Schilder (1935). The term body image refers to the preconscious or conscious qualities of the various body functions and body appearances.

Looking more closely at the relation between the two concepts, several distinct differences appear. The body ego, as the basic ego matrix lacking distinct verbalizable qualities, though endowed with psychic energy deriving from satisfactions and capable of functioning as a protorepresentation for dreams and other mental images (Spitz, 1955; Weil, 1970; Pacella, 1980), is as such always unconscious. It is derived from true fusional experiences and forms that part of the personality which remains in direct contact with the instinctual sources. The body ego is also a reservoir of that psychic energy which has been gained out of the id's fusional contact with the external world, as Freud schematically outlined. Furthermore, the body ego turns the instinctual drives to psychic experiences, but in a form which lacks distinct object relational features. It functions as a protoimage, screen, or matrix for more developed and true psychical representations.

The body image, on the other hand, is derived from more articulated interactions of the infant with significant objects or fantasies which interact with objects. The body image also undergoes many changes later in life, though the developmental years are clearly the most significant ones. Therefore the body image is a more articulated ego experience and relatively easily verbalizable, when it has once been cathected and activated in significant interactions with others or with fantasied goals and objects. Thus, the body image's tie to the instinctual is looser than that of the body ego. Adaptive changes occur much more easily in the body image than in the body ego (Elbirlik, 1980). The latter remains throughout life in an immediate relation to the body instincts.

A Clinical Vignette

In spite of success in her profession, Mrs. B, a 30-year-old teacher, felt uncertain and bewildered about herself, and sought psychoanalysis. Her current, second, marriage was unsatisfactory. She complained of not getting love, caresses, and admiration from her husband. She was the first child of her parents with three younger brothers, the next in age being eighteen months younger.

Very early on in the treatment she had a strange feeling with me which she did not fully understand at that time: There was something large and round between her and me which prevented natural contact between us. She was able to think only after more than five years of analytic work that her mother had been pregnant with a round belly and not able to hold her on her lap any longer when she was about to give birth to her brother. Later she became able to connect the transference image of me at the beginning of treatment to her experiences with her pregnant mother when she was still very small and badly needed her mother's presence and care. Her feeling about the round obstacle between her and me in the beginning of treatment was a kind of derivative of the Isakower phenomenon transformed to a more developed image of her pregnant mother.

As she began treatment, she started having intense wishes for physical intimacy. These caused problems in her relation with her husband who did not understand the intensity of her wishes. Disappointed in her husband, she sought a sexual relation with another man after her frustration had grown too intense for her to tolerate it, which coincided with a time when the treatment hours had been temporarily reduced due to my stay in another city. Later on she let her husband know about her affair which immediately caused a collapse in their relation and later a divorce. Only then did she turn herself fully to the analysis and begin to have sexual longings also for me. Among other things, she had a couple of openly sexual dreams about me which revealed her intense bodily wishes of being cared for and loved. Throughout the treatment she had significant weight problems and her body boundaries were unclear for a long time. She was also a hypochondriac and often felt compelled to eat something immediately after her analytic hour.

In the closing phase of her treatment she began to think about her sexual longings, that the sexual aspect was less significant than her wish to be cared for and satisfied by someone like a mother. Her relationship to both of her parents had been almost totally broken for many years since her early adolescence. She told many times how she despised both of them, especially her mother. After having been able to work through to a considerable degree her intense and repetitious frustrations which came from her relationship to her parents in the actuality of the transference, her relationship to them began to recover and she paid several successful visits home.

Her analytic story was one of significant narcissistic and exhibitionistic problems. It was also a story of her emotionally deprived and periodically severely conflictful childhood and relative abandonment. Her psychic economy was bound in a rather unchanged manner to her infantile bodily longings and body experiences at her mother's lap. One year before ending our joint work she gave me a small statue of a satisfied child lolling over a big ball, an image of a child's rest in the presence of a breast object. However, the tragic, at times even a dangerous, aspect in her life was connected with the collapse of her marriage. Her psychological working resources continued to be heavily weighed on by the marital problems in the treatment and they cast a shadow over the closing phase. She learned only at that time that her husband had had a regular relationship with another woman for several years and a child with this woman. Completing her analysis seemed to be a precondition for her to accept this frustrating reality and a further blow to her self-esteem.

Returning to the relation between the matrix of the body ego and the conscious–preconscious image of the body, it can be summarized that the body ego and body image stand to each other in a similar relation as the latent and manifest dream. Both maintain a contact with the bodily sources of the instincts, but the manifest body image contents cannot be "read out" as a kind of a direct text. Instead, the mental images of the body must be interpreted in relation to the current unconscious issues in order to arrive at their true meaning, in the same way as dream images have to be interpreted before their true latent content can be understood. In a similar way, the fragmentation of the body image which threatens to take place, for instance, in imminent psychosis, can be psychologically understood only through the unconscious threats to the latent body ego, which arise from unmanageable instinctual demands or problems related to loss of the primary object leading to organismic distress or panic.

In Table 2.1, I have summarized the main characteristics and differences between the body ego and the body image.

Toward Integration or Psychosis?

The primal psychological satisfactions involve merging of the self and the object. There is no boundary between the two in these experiences. Such satisfactions, otherwise greatly longed for, may become frightening and imply a threat to the very sense of existence. The wish for closeness and satisfaction may signify a danger, that the object (the breast) will be eaten and disappear, and the self may become swallowed by the object (Garma, 1955, 1974). Lewin's (1946) well-known oral triad "to eat, to be eaten, to die" describes the same thing (L. Reiser, 1990). The absence of the boundary between the self and the object may lead to the opposite of satisfaction of all kinds. The primitive anxieties arising from these threats may be activated

TABLE 2.1

The Character of the Body Ego in Relation to the Body Image

	Body Ego	Body Image
Origin	Fusion of skin-mucosa with mother-milk Function of affect and perception	Experience and fantasy of body appearance, function and movement in relation to mother and father objects No actual fusion
Source	Bodily sensations under direct influence from the instincts Breast feeding, sexual experiences "Where id was, there ego shall be" (Freud)	Affects related to the appearance and function of the body in different developmental stages (oral, locomotor, anal, urethral-phallic, inner-genital, genital reorganization in adolescence) Contact with the instincts mediated by affects and images
Psychical Character	Unconscious, nonverbal Preideational, matrix or screen for mental contents proper	Conscious and preconscious, verbal and nonverbal Fantasy connected, ideational
Nature of Affect	Tension and relief Satisfaction/lack of satisfaction of hunger, sexual, and other drives	Variable sensations and feelings of the body self connected with neutralized pleasure or a fear of loss of pleasure
Nature of Object Relationship	Fusion Body ego matrix can be activated in primitive separation-related object and transference constellations, accompanied often by a feeling of an "impasse" and frustration	No fusion Pleasure and mastery of the body self related to objects and fantasies about them
Symbolic Function	Protosymbol, protoself Matrix (screen) for symbols proper	Symbols equal to any other psychological symbols (dreams, mental images, neurotic symptoms)

in various separation experiences, which reinforce the longing for oneness as an escape from the separation.

If the early self experience is able to retain its pleasurable
character, the activation of the early body ego states involves
a reassurance of a primitive kind (Spitz, 1955; Boyer, 1960;
and Pacella, 1980), among others. Such early experiences will
then reaffirm the absences of any cause for separation anxiety due to the merger-quality of the body ego feelings. Therefore, more common than a psychotic outcome, the Isakower
experience and other phenomena related to it, do generally
indicate a reassuring conviction, that the threatening separation is not a reality. The body ego can function in this way as
a reservoir of a primitive, reassuring sense of existence.

The activation of these phenomena during treatment
seems to be capable of reinforcing a search for new object
cathexes. When the working through process has advanced
far enough and resolved sufficiently splits of object cathexes,
the more deeply seated body ego matrix may become newly
available and get activated in the transference. An example
of this has been vividly described by Volkan (1975). Boyer
(1960) has described the activation of the dream screen in
analysis of two different patients with a clinical disturbance
on the level of schizophrenia and borderline disorder. The
narcissistic organization of the self when changing toward
true object relations leads to the activation of the dream
screen in circumstances when loss of the newly gained object relation is threatened. The dream screen initiates a double
cathexis of the analyst as a narcissistic projected object and
as a real person.

Also Rycroft (1951) has mentioned revitalization of current
object relations in a patient, who began to experience dream
screenlike elements as part of the current transference fantasy. We may assume that the inherent link between self and
object within the body ego formation has been freed under
such circumstances and therefore becomes capable of supporting the search for new objects.

A Clinical Vignette

Miss H, who had sought analysis after several failures in her previous treatment efforts, began to have short dreamy states, when we had been working together for about three years. The dreamy states were experienced by her as uncontrollable break-throughs which were not unpleasant, but made her somewhat bewildered. They could occur both during the analytic session and outside it. At the same time, during a weekend trip, she had an impulsive relationship with a man completely unknown to her. She described him to me in such a way that it made me think that it dealt with an aspect of the current transference. After my interpretation of this, her anxiety diminished and she had several episodes of heavy sleepiness during the sessions and repeated weak breakthroughs of dreamy states also out-side the treatment which were different from her ordinary sleepiness. They were like miniature Isakower/dream screen phenomena, which she easily reported to me without any ref-erence to their content. They were like short blank dreams. At the same time, there was an observable increase in her rest-fulness and ability to work psychologically.

The Body Ego and the Symptoms of Schizophrenia

Research evidence is accumulating that a combination of genetic–biological factors and pathological psychological in-teractions is at work in the pathogenesis of a schizophrenic psychosis. Psychological and biological factors interact when a schizophrenic breakdown is about to occur (Tienari et al., 1994). We have, however, insufficient knowledge of how the interaction of biological and psychological factors takes place. The basic link within the body ego, that between perception and affect, may play a role in the precipitation of a schizo-phrenic psychosis, specifically, a role in the breakdown of that crucial link within the body ego, which keeps perception from without and the vital affects from within together by way of the bond arising from the fusion of the two in the primal satisfactions (Lehtonen, 1994).

The firmness of the perceptual–affective link depends on both of its formative factors, the perception *and* the affect. The affective satisfactory responses arising in the infant are modulated by the individual's idiosyncratic, biologically and genetically tailored mode of responding. On the other hand, the bond is equally and simultaneously dependent on the appropriate or inappropriate nature of the mother's way of meeting and responding to the infant's needs at a given moment. The body ego matrix forms in this way a milieu where the constitution and the environment meet and interact for promoting or disturbing the development of the infant's mental health.

Also Easson (1973, p. 73) and Hoffer (1981, p. 43) connect the predisposition to psychosis with the early (body) ego state, which remains split and separated to unintegrated ego nuclei when the necessary loving handling has been lacking. The outbreak of the productive schizophrenic symptoms seems to deal with a breakdown of this primary link within the body ego, the intactness of which would be of utmost importance for normal psychic economy. The breaking of the primary link results in a disintegration of the internal and external constituents of the psyche, a split on the most primary level of the psychic structures, more primary than any of the better known splitting processes characteristic of borderline and narcissistic disturbances.

Many of the symptoms of schizophrenia do indeed indicate a disturbance or even a total loss of the vital cathecting functions of the body ego. Hallucinations indicate that there are perceptual processes going on, which totally lack a cathexis that would generate meaning and satisfaction to them. The required link between affective experience and the perceptual processes has fallen apart resulting in uncathected internal perceptions which are experienced as real perceptions coming from without. At the moment they occur they have no connection to the other parts of the mind and are therefore void of meaning and affect.

The impaired functioning of the body ego in schizophrenia is evident also in the inability of the patient, especially in acute stages, to tolerate separation, calm down, fall asleep, have dreams, and enjoy rest. All of these functions are disturbed in acute schizophrenia suggesting that the capacity to regulate the basic, vital psychic functions and economy is fundamentally out of order.

Comparing hypnagogic hallucinations described by Isakower with hallucinations in schizophrenia shows clear differences between them. The former have retained their vital body cathexis and they are in fact not true hallucinations. The hypnagogic experiences are a part of a more integrated psychological functioning, even though they are unexplained for the subject at the time of their occurrence due to their unconscious, nonverbal character. They remain within a relatively integrated psychological experience and can be memorized, observed, and scrutinized freely when they are occurring. They can also be communicated in a reflective way according to the will, which means that the reality testing function remains intact during them. They are not accompanied by ego-alien projections as schizophrenic hallucinations are, and their relation to other similar kinds of phenomena within the mind, such as ordinary dreams, is evident. All this indicates that the psychological cathexis of the hypnagogic perceptions remains unimpaired in clear contrast to the split and noncathected hallucinatory perceptions in schizophrenic psychosis.

Rosenfeld (1992) stresses the loss of the psychological body boundaries, the primitive, fluid, and completely undifferentiated nature of the core of the psychotic body experience, often rationalized as blood or some other liquid or mass, the loss of the psychologically meaningful tie of the body experiences to objects and environment, and the paranoid and delusional thoughts ensuing from this. Volkan's (1995) fresh conceptualization and the rich clinical description of schizophrenia from the point of view of an adult and infantile part of the psychotic self, gives further clinical support to the relevance of the approach to schizophrenia from the level of developmentally early and primitive layers of the mind as described by Volkan in chapter 1.

Conclusions

Conceptualizing the ego first and foremost as a body ego was a central part of Freud's formulations when he delineated the structural theory. The basic assumptions about the body ego were left schematic by him, however, and he described its role in an almost aphoristic manner as the psychical projection of the body surface. His view of the role of the body ego in the general ego development implied that there was in the beginning a *real contact* between bodily and mental phenomena, but the nature of it has remained unspecified.

The relation of the body ego concept to other metapsychological and developmental viewpoints is not well understood. The trauma of birth has had traditionally, and especially in the early days of psychoanalysis, a relatively important role as the primal source of trauma and anxiety response. During more recent times the psychological impact of changes following the cessation of intrauterine life, birth, and the beginning of infancy has not been studied with equal interest. However, the changes brought about by the birth are great not only physiologically, but also psychologically. A complete dependence of the infant on an external object is implemented, but the infant does not have any ready-made psychological capacities to adapt to the new and vital dependence on the mother. Therefore it is natural that the life-giving satisfactions the infant receives from the mother, particularly in breast-feeding or surrogate satisfactions, bring about a basis for an entirely new kind of psychology compared to the elementary perceptions and experiences that are possible in utero.

Breast-feeding entails a fusion between the infant and the mother in the mouth–nipple and skin contact. There also arises in successful breast-feeding a fusion between the elementary bodily affects of satisfaction with the concomitant sense impressions in the infant. It is natural to assume that the psychic projection of the surface experience, as Freud delineated the origin of the body ego, is brought about specifically by such vital experiences involving fusion between self and object and affect and perception. Freud's basic formulation becomes endowed with alive, vital, and primordial psychology when it is approached from the point of view of the early caretaking and especially the most vital and satisfying aspects of it.

Seeing the birth of the ego as a result of such fusional satisfactions is supported also by clinical data in patients who have experienced the complex of hypnagogic phenomena evoking reminiscences of breast-feeding, as described by Isakower, and developed further by Lewin into the dream screen concept. By identifying the body ego with the primordial layer-structure of the psyche as displayed in Isakower and dream screen phenomena, the somewhat enigmatic concept of the body ego can be better placed in the general psychoanalytic theory of early ego development, and understood as a part of the archaic modes of psychological functioning also in adults.

Neurophysiological support can be given to the assumption that breast-feeding leaves evidence of the infant's early psychophysiological patterns and primordial modes of experiencing in a fashion that have a founding role in the earliest layers of the psyche. Freud's statement that the ego is born when the id comes into contact with the outside world, finds its natural prototype in breast-feeding as the psychological "site" for the nascent body ego. It is a natural outcome of such primary satisfactions as breast-feeding, since the ego traces precipitating from such experiences are products of a vital, pleasurable satisfaction.

In the description of the hypnagogic and dream phenomena by Isakower and Lewin the peculiar affective character of the early experiences gains some clarification. The dominant modality of the body ego affect extends itself between tension and relief, varying in its quality and intensity according to the state of the satisfaction of the primordial bodily needs. The latter distinguish themselves clearly from ordinary object related affects both in their nature and in their unconscious, nonverbal character. Body ego becomes in this landscape that psychological structure which regulates the psychophysiological states of the vital satisfactions, tension relief, sleep, and basic welfare. Body ego is born in a direct contact with the instincts and remains so for the rest of the life. Also the origin of repression can be investigated as a part of the maintenance of the nascent body ego boundaries.

While the object relation bringing about the primordial body ego is fusional in its nature, the share of the object and infant in the outcome, that is, in the fusional pleasure experience, can be differentiated only artificially. In the nascent state of the body ego the contribution of self and object are indistinguishable. Interestingly, this seems to be an analogous relation that prevails normally in dreams between self and object representations, which are interchangeable and show loss of object constancy while dreaming.

Though functioning as a resource of psychic energy and as the prime psychological site of satisfaction and rest, the body ego experiences when activated clinically after the infancy period, can turn out to be threatening due to their fusional and undifferentiated nature. Confusion between object and self may be imminent and the possibility of loss or annihilation of a differentiated self experience may become a reality. The body ego experiences which are normally ego supporting, may then change into a threatening entryway to an undifferentiated psychotic world. In schizophrenia an even more profound breakdown occurs in the functioning of the body ego. The basic link between affect and perception tends to disintegrate resulting in noncathected, split experiences of real hallucinations and delusions.

The body ego may thus be seen as a natural psychological "meeting place" and a context for binding together the impacts of nature and nurture. While the latest theories of the origin of schizophrenia emphasize the role of both, it seems feasible to place the interaction between nature and nurture at the early protopsychological events between the newborn infant's responses and the impact of the kind of caretaking the infant is met with.

The points made are illustrated by several clinical vignettes of adolescent and adult nonpsychotic patients, which may give an opportunity to discuss the relation between body ego and the other closely related concept, body image. The latter is a set of body attached mental images which are preconscious or conscious, whereas the body ego is as such always nonverbal and unconscious. Their relation (body image/body ego) is analogous to the relation between the manifest and the latent dream. In order to get a grasp of the clinically relevant issues of the body ego layer of experiencing, requires consequently, that the apparent messages of the conscious–preconscious body images have to be interpreted and traced back to the latent body ego issues.

The body ego is in itself a protosymbol and functions as a blank matrix for symbols proper. The latter are created from the primordial blank matrix of the body ego through experiences in object relations. Lack of love and good handling in infancy create a predisposition at the level of the body ego to a psychotic breakdown of the primal selfobject representations. This is because the early fundamental bond between affect and perception remains weak and the mental images poorly integrated.

References

Abse, W. (1977), The dream screen: Phenomenon and noumenon. *Psychoanal. Quart.*, 46:256–286.

Boyer, L. B. (1960), A hypothesis regarding the time of appearance of the dream screen. *Internat. J. Psycho-Anal.*, 41:114–122.

Dann, O. T. (1992), The Isakower phenomenon revisited. A case study. *Internat. J. Psycho-Anal.*, 73:481–491.

Davis, M., & Wallbridge, D. (1981), *Boundary and Space*. London: Karnac Books.

Easson, W. M. (1973), The earliest ego development primitive memory traces, and the Isakower phenomenon. *Psychoanal. Quart.*, 42:60–72.

Elbirlik, K. (1980), Organ loss, grieving and itching. *Amer. J. Psychother.*, 34:523–533.

Enckell, M. (1988), Psychoanalysis and the Jewish tradition. *Scand. Psychoanal. Rev.*, 11:111–159.

Fink, G. (1967), Analysis of the Isakower phenomenon. *J. Amer. Psychoanal. Assn.*, 15:281–293.

Freud, S. (1900), The Interpretation of Dreams. *Standard Edition*, 4 & 5. London: Hogarth Press, 1953.

——— (1915), Repression. *Standard Edition*, 14:141–158. London: Hogarth Press, 1957.

——— (1923), The Ego and the Id. *Standard Edition*, 19:1–59. London: Hogarth Press, 1961.

——— (1940), An Outline of Psychoanalysis. *Standard Edition*, 23:139–207. London: Hogarth Press, 1964.

Furman, E. (1992), *Toddlers and Their Mothers*. New York: International Universities Press.

Gammill, J. (1980), Some reflections on analytic listening and the dream screen. *Internat. J. Psycho-Anal.*, 61:375–381.

Garma, A. (1955), Vicissitudes of the dream screen and the Isakower phenomenon. *Psychoanal. Quart.*, 24:369–382.

——— (1974), *The Psychoanalysis of Dreams*. New York: Jason Aronson.

Gediman, H. K. (1971), The concept of stimulus barrier: Its review and formulation as an adaptive ego function. *Internat. J. Psycho-Anal.*, 52:243–257.

Glenn, I. (1993), Developmental transformations: The Isakower phenomenon as an example. *J. Amer. Psychoanal. Assn.*, 41:1113–1134.

Greenspan, S. I. (1992), *Infancy and Early Childhood: The Practice of Clinical Assessment and Intervention with Emotional and Developmental Challenges*. Madison, CT: International Universities Press.

Greenacre, P. (1952), The biological economy of birth. In: *Trauma, Growth and Personality*, ed. P. Greenacre. New York: International Universities Press, 1980, pp. 3–26.

Hagglund, T. B., & Piha, H. (1980), The inner space of the body image. *Psychoanal. Quart.*, 49:256–283.

Heilbrunn, G. (1953), Fusion of the Isakower phenomenon with the dream screen. *Psychoanal. Quart.*, 22:200–204.

Hoffer, W. (1981), *Early Development and Education of the Child*. London: Hogarth Press.

Isakower, O. (1938), A contribution to the patho-physiology of phenomena associated with falling asleep. *Internat. J. Psycho-Anal.*, 19:331–345.

Kanzer, M. (1954), Observations on blank dreams with orgasms. *Psychoanal. Quart.*, 23:511–520.

Kepecs, I. G. (1952), A waking screen analogous to the dream screen. *Psychoanal. Quart.*, 21:167–171.

Lehtonen, J. (1980), The relationship between neurophysiology and psychoanalysis in the light of dream research. *Perspect. Biolog. Med.*, 23:415–423.

———— (1991), The body ego from the point of view of psychophysical fusion. *Psychother. & Psychosom.*, 56:30–35.

———— (1994), From dualism to psychobiological interaction. A comment on the study by Dr. Tienari and his coworkers. *Brit. J. Psychiatry*, 164 (suppl. 23):27–28.

Leira, T. (1995), Silence and communication: Nonverbal dialogue and therapeutic action. *Scand. Psychoanal. Rev*, 18:41–65.

Lewin, B. D. (1946), Sleep, the mouth, and the dream screen. *Psychoanal. Quart.*, 15:119–134.

———— (1948), Inferences from the dream screen. *Internat. J. Psycho-Anal.*, 29:73–97.

———— (1953), Reconsideration of the dream screen. *Psychoanal. Quart.*, 22:174–199.

———— (1955), Dream psychology and the analytic situation. *Psychoanal. Quart.*, 24:169–199.

McDougall, J. (1989), *Theatres of the Body: A Psychoanalytical Approach to Psychosomatic Illness.* New York: W. W. Norton.

Mahler, M., Pine, F., & Bergman, A. (1975), *The Psychological Birth of the Human Infant.* New York: Basic Books.

Pacella, B. L. (1980), The primal matrix configuration. In: *Rapprochement: The Critical Subphase of Separation–Individuation,* ed. R. F. Lax, S. Bach, & J. A. Burland. New York: Jason Aronson.

Piontelli, A. (1988), Prenatal life and birth as reflected in the analysis of a 2-year-old psychiatric girl. *Internat. Rev. Psycho-Anal.*, 15:73–81.

———— (1989), A study of twins before and after birth. *Internat. Rev. Psycho-Anal.*, 16:413–426.

Reiser, L. W. (1990), The oral triad and the bulimic quintet. Understanding the bulimic episode. *Internat. Rev. Psycho-Anal.*, 17:239–248.

Reiser, M. F. (1990), *Memory in Mind and Brain: What Dream Imagery Reveals.* New York: Basic Books.

Richards, A. D. (1985), Isakower-like experience on the couch: A contribution to the psychoanalytic understanding of regressive ego phenomena. *Psychoanal. Quart.*, 54:415–434.

Rosenfeld, D. (1992), *The Psychotic Aspects of the Personality.* London: Karnac Books.

Rycroft, C. (1951), A contribution to the study of the dream screen. *Internat. J. Psycho-Anal.*, 32:178–184.

Salonen, S. (1979), On the metapsychology of schizophrenia. *Internat. J. Psycho-Anal.*, 60:73–81.

Schilder, P. (1935), *The Image and Appearance of the Human Body.* New York: International Universities Press.

Scott, W. C. M. (1948), Some embryological, neurological, psychiatric and psycho-analytic implications of the body science. *Internat. J. Psycho-Anal.*, 29:141–155.

———— (1985), Narcissism, the body, phantasy, fantasy, internal and external objects and the "Body Scheme." *J. Melanie Klein Soc.*, 3:23–49.

Sperling, O. E. (1957), A psychoanalytic study of hypnagogic hallucinations. *J. Amer. Psychoanal. Assn.*, 5:115–123.

Spitz, R. A. (1955), The primal cavity: A contribution to the genesis of perception and its role for psychoanalytic theory. *The Psychoanalytic Study of the Child*, 10:215–240. New York: International Universities Press.

———— (1957), *No and Yes.* New York: International Universities Press.

———— (1959), *A Genetic Field Theory of Ego Formation.* New York: International Universities Press.

———— Emde, R. E., & Metcalf, O. R. (1970), Further prototypes of ego formation. A working paper from a research project on early development. *The Psychoanalytic Study of the Child*, 25:417–441. New York: International Universities Press.

Stern, D. (1985), *The Interpersonal World of the Infant.* New York: Basic Books.

Tähkä, V. (1993), *The Mind and Its Treatment.* New York: International Universities Press.

Tienari, P. J., Wynne, L. C., Moring, J., Lahti, I., Naarala, M., Sorri, A., Wahlberg, K. E., Saarento, O., Seitamaa, M., Kaleva, M., Laksy, K. (1994), The Finnish Adoptive Family Study of Schizophrenia: Implications for family research. *Brit. J. Psychiatry*, 164 (suppl. 23):20–26.

Vauhkonen, K. (1990), On the initial stage of psychic experience. *Scand. Psychoanal. Rev*, 13:16–31.

Volkan, V. D. (1975), Cosmic laughter: A study of primitive splitting. In: *Tactics and Techniques of Psychoanalytic Psychotherapy*, Vol. 2, ed. P. L. Giovannini, New York: Jason Aronson, pp. 425–440.

———— (1995), *The Infantile Psychotic Self and Its Fates: Understanding and Treating of Schizophrenics and Other Difficult Patients.* Northvale, NJ: Jason Aronson.

Weil, A. (1970), The basic core. *The Psychoanalytic Study of the Child*, 25:442–460. New York: International Universities Press.

Winnicott, D. W. (1971), *Playing and Reality.* London: Tavistock Publications.

3

Humiliation and Dignity: Reflections on Ego Integrity

SIMO SALONEN, M.D.

In Bernardo Bertolucci's film *The Last Emperor* (1987), the eunuchs, who formed the servant body of the imperial court of China, were expelled from the Forbidden City because of their deceit. In leaving the city, they walked in single file, each of them carrying an urn that contained his own sexual organs. When the wives of the Emperor wondered about the slowly moving procession, an adviser told them the hidden meaning of the ceremony: "Whatever their crimes, they cannot be deprived of their right to be buried as a whole man." This extremely condensed scene illuminates my topic in a flash; the problem of human dignity is deeply rooted in the unconscious conflicts and instinctual dangers. Also Bertolucci's idea of becoming integrated in facing one's death deserves to be studied more closely.

In my previous studies on psychic trauma I came to the idea that the experience of one's dignity and the capacity for psychic representation belong together (Salonen, 1989, 1992). Now, I will develop this idea further. In carrying their genitals with them during the ceremony, Bertolucci's eunuchs were able to find a symbolic representation for their tragic loss: castration. Being deprived of this opportunity would have meant an irreparable loss of their dignity.

Within the Danger Zone; A Case Study

Mrs. D came into analysis after having realized that she was unable to control her panic reactions. Two years before, she had completed a lengthy psychotherapy with me. In fact, she had not lived many years of her adult life without some kind of psychotherapeutic support; she was 45 years old when we began the analysis. In addition, she was in regular need of medical help because of psychosomatic problems. She desperately needed other people, professionals as well as friends to protect her vulnerable self. She was worried about her marriage and the future of her children. In social life, Mrs. D was a very successful academically trained professional, with special interest in the business world.

Instead of following the sequential course of the analysis, which lasted over eight years, I have chosen some episodes that are relevant for my study. Her case makes clear how the maintenance of one's dignity can be endangered from within.

Mrs. D's inner world surprisingly simulated the calamities of her mother's life. Actually, her analysis brings to mind what has been written about the children of Holocaust survivors (Klein and Kogan, 1986). Her mother's first marriage, which resulted in divorce, was a nightmare. Both of her children died before their third year, and, in addition, she had at least one miscarriage; her first husband also died. She remarried, and about the time of the analysand's birth, the mother had fallen ill with rheumatic fever, and was unable to breast-feed her baby. Mrs. D was to remain an only child.

Encapsulated Trauma

The mother's inability to breast-feed her baby was only the beginning of the hardships to come. At the age of one year and two months, the child was sent to a pediatric hospital, two hundred kilometers from home; it happened again when she was 5 years old. The reason for the hospitalizations, lasting two months each, were digestive symptoms and unexplained fever.

In view of this background, it is no wonder that her life was dominated by an extensive sadomasochistic struggle and constant dread of rejection. Her analysis reminds me of McDougall's work with psychosomatic patients. The analysand not only felt herself traumatically rejected, but, at the same time, she also shared, very concretely, the experience of fusion with her mother: "one body for two," in suffering (McDougall, 1989). Chasseguet-Smirgel's (1985a,b, 1992) ideas on anality and falsehood are also relevant for my study. On the whole, Mrs. D's analysis reflects her constant struggle for psychic survival. In fact, the problem of dignity is closely related to this struggle. After two years of analysis the analysand's acting out behavior became accentuated. After having been up to that point a more or less submissive person and also a devoted proponent of high ethical values, she found herself adopting cold, even harsh behavior in business life, often without the slightest feelings of guilt. In behaving toward me according to these same principles, she often made me feel helpless and vulnerable in maintaining the analytical stance. When I once referred to her cynicism, she associated it with a black capsule in her mind. Then she went on: "What is enclosed is cold hatred. It is like dangerous radiation, the lack of affect. . . . It would be absolutely impossible to approach this area without the intruder being destroyed." The analysis had reached her inner danger zone.

In the following session, Mrs. D was convinced that the capsule not only made her treat other people harshly, but also caused her analysis to continue endlessly. She said: "It forms a clearly demarcated area in the garden of my mind. My split is there. Keeping this area separated is my original lie. If this lie can be maintained, the capsule will not disturb me either." The analysand had often experienced me, as well as her husband, as a lifeless lump. At this time, she felt the lump to be within, not outside any more. She proceeded:

> The last contact with the encapsulated area was cut when my father died. I then lost my hope. That is why we cannot do anything for it. . . . My hospital stay occurs to me, at the age of one, and then at the age of 5. After returning home, my father was the only human being left. He was left outside my cold hatred. . . . Is it possible that hope can be found within the capsule?

In the following session the analysand was infuriated because I had detected her secret. She was no longer able to keep the content of the capsule segregated. She said that she could empathize with adolescents who burglarize and steal, and then destroy everything. She also accused me of being mechanical toward her: "The major part of you is reserved for the other patients. When I at last give you a gift, my capsule, you offer me nothing in return." Upon my asking if she had been annoyed with her mother's intrusiveness in the same way as with my interpretations, she replied: "Exactly, you always poke your nose into my affairs to find out whether I received enemas from my mother, but you never tell me if your mother did the same to you." Maybe the analysis had not only revealed her ego split, but, initially, also her great secret, which she had kept from her mother, the daughter's love for the father.

Half a year later the experience of deadly radiation became linked to the feeling of guilt that was related to masturbation. In this phase, she felt that I was the source of dangerous radiation, causing her somatic ills. I had to represent the archaic superego aspect in the transference.

Silent trauma beyond her acting out became more under-standable some weeks later when her elderly mother had been taken to hospital because of serious heart trouble. In this phase, her guilt feelings were extremely acute. In talking about her inability to feel sorrow in the face of the mother's approaching death, I found myself saying that being frustrated is no sin. In coming to the next session, she was very impressed:

Last time I was completely reluctant to consider my mother's death. Then, at the end of the session, something peculiar happened, after your having said that being frustrated is no sin. I felt myself being absolutely alone, without any people around. Pain and desolation belong to this state. The good Samaritan occurs to me, but what differs is that in the Biblical parable there were still other people around. The robbery still occurred! My experience was like listening to distant traffic noise, without any affect. . . . There was no time. . . . Might the word *autistic* signify this state? It must relate to a very early experience, I think. There was no hope, but I was not hopeless either. Being hopeless means already feeling. There was no blaming there. It feels strange, but I do not accuse my mother anymore. Being in this state is nobody's fault. One only gets into it.

I repeated that being frustrated is no sin. She went on:

It is no use waiting for a noble prince to rescue you. What matters is that one only stays in this state. I have not understood that my parents have done their best. . . . This does not at all fit into what I am used to thinking about myself. I have considered myself to be a person capable of deeds, both good and bad. . . . I am not willing to integrate such a great help-lessness into myself. . . .

She had just previously experienced a minor surgical operation. She realized that it had been unfounded from the medical point of view, and that this act manifested an urge to free herself of extreme helplessness.

When the analysis then proceeded, she became more and more aware of shame related to her means of avoiding psychic trauma. Also the history of this avoidance was reconstructed. In staying in the hospital a second time, she had invented, together with another little girl, an exciting fantasy world, "the forbidden forest" where exciting horrors stimulated their minds. The question was not only her sadomasochistic self-stimulation, but at the same time also her belief that she could actually control the traumatic circumstances by omnipotent means. To be then revealed at this point was extremely shameful for her.

In fact, the unconsciously inflicted sadomasochistic excitement and the belief in being able to manipulate reality, including death, formed the core of Mrs. D's resistance. In the course of a laborious working through process, this fortification surrendered little by little. A session from the sixth year of analysis illustrates this transformation:

She used the word *spell* to denote the pathological excitement which she was addicted to. At the beginning of the session, she came back to her spell:

> It simply disappeared last week, but this is not easier either. I feel horror and think suicide would be an instant solution. . . . I am reading poetry and weeping all the time. Now I have contact with my emotions. The bubbles have been pricked. This fear is my original dread. . . . I am starting to see reality. (Pause) Only a shell came back from the hospital, brisk and similar-looking. Now I would like to destroy it, too.

Daughter and Her Mother

After two years of analysis she came to understand that her complicated relationships with men had a deep undercurrent of unconscious attachment to the female body, the realization of which she had resisted fiercely. In the succeeding analysis, we could reconstruct her sensual longing for the mother's intimacy and her breasts. For example, she could have nearly hallucinatory sensations of milk taste in her mouth.

What is highly interesting is that her psychosomatic problems became more understandable at the same time. As long as she could remember, she had been suffering from migraine, colitis, and recurrent infections. The most serious problem at the time, was, however, incipient arthrosis that, fortunately, stopped progressing. But it gave us an opportunity to observe how the primordial ego may function in the midst of life-threatening early circumstances. The defensive methods used were based on magical omnipotence. For example, she experienced me as radiating healing energy, and, after a while, she could imagine me possessing the power to destroy her bodily health. In this phase she also resorted to all kinds of paramedical treatments and idle quackery to control the progression of destruction in her body, arthrosis.

Mrs. D introduced a session from this period by telling about magnets she was wearing on her skin, and a strict vegetarian diet. The whole previous night she had spent counting money. In asking whether her intention was to control her own body in this way, she responded: "On the contrary, I hope that you will feed me and also take care of my body. Taste of milk occurs to me. . . . When you say 'we,' it feels great. . . . Now the magnets are yours, not my own. I want to merge." Perhaps it was not mere chance that she began to understand at the end of the same session the background of one of her major problems, namely, her endless desire to maximize profit in business, regardless of the means used. It represented her urge to exploit the early mother.

Three years later she came back to her desire for bodily intimacy, after having met me out on the town, by chance. This incident had been a very shocking experience for her because she imagined that I had perceived her hidden love for me in her glance. In the next session, the analysis took the following course:

If someone touches me, I am like molten wax. By the way, do you know the poem *Touch of Evil*, the bad guys earn their lot. . . . This is to disparage what I told about my love for you yesterday. It's a matter of indifference now, because you will never touch me . . . if only someone evil would do it, at least . . . pain, murderer. I can't live without somebody touching me. (We knew, that the Finnish word *koskea*, touch, signifies also feeling pain.)

I would like to select one more session from the last stage of the analysis, because it leads us into the eye of the patient's inner hurricane.

After having been informed about a colleague's fatal cancer, she came to think about her own early trauma that had led her close to inner death: "If the skin contact is lost, there is no contact left. . . . Then the skin will get charred. . . . The contact is mediated by the skin only, and partially also by the voice." I commented on her fragmentary train of thought by saying that only skin contact is reassuring enough for an infant, and losing it denotes pain. She continued: "First comes pain caused by desire, the whole skin is longing. Then comes cold, burning sensation . . . cold radiation, cold warmness, nuclear energy."

We shall now return to a remarkable incident that took place in the middle phase of our work. Mrs. D's elderly mother then asked her daughter to tell the analyst that a woman who has lost three of her children to death cannot bring up a child in a better way. I think the mother's message indicated that she had been able, not long before her actual death, to integrate her own traumas without unbearable guilt. The other point is that the mother thought this matter to be of importance for her daughter's analysis.

After her mother's death, I once asked if the mother had possibly been caring for her dead daughter in her living child, in order to avoid the painful experience of her children dying. Mrs. D responded: "As long as I can remember, our relationship has been a losing battle. We were clinging to each other to avoid death. Death was actual." I proceeded that perhaps her idea of destruction within her own body was also related to the dead half-sister. She replied: "I have wanted to eliminate it by surgical operations. I feel it everywhere. . . ." In the following sessions she returned to the same theme:

> We shared pain and death, my mother and me. First it feels sweet, but then the faces become crueler and crueler. Which of us will be taken first? In being together we are in safety, no separation. . . . This sounds incredible. My father is right outside all of this. His death was therefore so painful for me. He represented hope. . . . It feels unbelievable that I am living, although my mother is dead.

The mother's psychic trauma, the children dying, formed one aspect of Mrs. D's early world of perception. The other aspect was her own oral frustration and hunger for bodily intimacy. We can now understand that she had great difficulties in dealing with her instinctual turmoil at the psychic level. After having failed in this respect, her helpless ego had resorted to destructive maternal fusion, in which pain, acting out, and somatization form the last bridgehead of survival.

The Ego Split

Early psychic trauma was a powerful source of deep resistance in this analysis. On the other hand, the ego split formed the main obstacle against integrating the traumatic area. It was in her ego's interest not to see and not to hear that which was obvious. In facing reality, she always left her own reservations, carefully concealed and often brilliantly rationalized. On the other hand, she has also retained a genuine contact with reality. That is why she knew herself to be concealing the truth. Her basic strategy was to keep these ego aspects apart in order to avoid realizing her helplessness vis-à-vis the instinctual

dangers, separation, castration, and loss of love. To preserve
the belief in her omnipotence, she had resorted to an intellectual compromise.

To avoid castration anxiety she had erected an anal phallus, forming the unconscious core of her omnipotence fantasy. It became analyzed toward the end of the seventh year:

We had been dealing with her inclination to lie. The following day she felt herself to be absolutely rotten and mortally ill.
In my referring to the previous session, she said: "Lying is ex-
clusively your problem, not mine." I replied that perhaps it is
easier to identify the problem in me. Mrs. D proceeded by talking about her dread of looking at the penis. After my asking if
her feeling ill could signify a punishment for doing this, perhaps a death sentence, she continued: "It feels as if the death
sentence has already been passed. . . . You can't do nothing
anyway. My illnesses indicate how little your penis actually is!"
I said that she seemed to be doubtful about my ability to pen-
etrate into her problem, her difficulty in looking at the penis.
She went on: "Lying means that I am lying to myself that I have
not seen it. All other lies are absolutely secondary. The death
sentence feels wrong, because I have hardly seen anything."
In referring to the possibility of her having seen her naked
father, she associated this with the sauna:

> A tremendously big one, brown like poo-poo. . . . It is not at
> all the same the men have, but more like what I imagine the
> trolls possessing. It is not a part of anything, but a detached
> one. This feels tremendously forbidden . . . related to bad.
> The ordinary penis is related to good. . . . Now I realize that
> this is the tumor that I have always wanted to have removed,
> in order to begin my ordinary life.

From then on, the atmosphere was changed when her
manipulative use of transference made room for genuine
oedipal desire. At the same time her feminine vulnerability
came to the fore.

Confronting an audience had always been extremely difficult for the analysand. In once giving a speech, she realized
that she had changed lately in this respect: "I feel that something more stable has been established between the stage and
my fear." I referred to the split in her sense of reality: On the
one hand she felt herself to be a sufficiently good professional,
but on the other hand she experienced herself as totally worthless. Mrs. D proceeded by telling me that in feeling worthless,
she feels the scorn of her female colleagues: "It is a sensation
at the front of my body, from my genitals to the neck. I am used
to bending down to protect my front. It feels like the normal
skin would have been replaced by a thin sensitive surface, or
sore skin." In my linking this sensation with genital masturbation, the analysand agreed, seemingly relieved.

Two months later she was extremely bewildered after having lost her handbag:

> It feels like something is missing or fading away. I am in ter-
> rible need of permanence, that a thing can be found where
> it was . . . I am losing control. I can't remember what has ac-
> tually been happening . . . a total amnesia regarding my hand
> bag. Perhaps you are able to create a world without this hu-
> miliation.

Her anxiety bore, originally, the stamp of early psychic
trauma, subjecting her not only to sadomasochistic suffering,
but also to accentuated panic in confronting the unconscious
idea of castration in the outside world. However, the reconstruction of the ego split in the transference with the understanding of its defensive nature had made the working
through of the original castration shock possible.

Structural Conflict

I will bring my case report to a close by examining how the
analysand's inner danger zone became finally bound within

a larger structural context in her mind. My material as a whole suggests that the most destructive forces opposing analytical progress are related not only to a breach in the primary identification, psychic trauma; they also relate to the superego that decisively amplifies its effects.

After two years of analysis, I became confronted, unexpectedly, with her acting out behavior. The incident was related to another patient of mine, whom she knew, which of course left me very vulnerable in the situation. I reacted to her act with spontaneous anger without being able to control myself. This incident brought her violent superego conflict into the analysis. Until then it had been concealed behind the analysand's submissiveness. Her initial reaction to my anger was intolerable pain, which was then followed by withdrawal into a desolate state of mind. What then occurred to her was her father's wrath in the bathroom when she was a child.

Two weeks later, she was able to analyze the dramatic incident more closely. "At the moment of your anger, the same change took place in my mind as during the last days in hospital. In that state the other people don't count anymore." I said perhaps this state of mind had already made her incapable of entering into my other patient's situation and of understanding my devotion to my work. She proceeded: "I often speak about you like a lifeless object. I abandon you as I do all other people, before they will do the same for me. Your anger meant rejection for me. The point is that I thought you would react as I am used to do. . . ." Toward the end of the same session, for the first time she got in touch with the idea of sibling rivalry.

Regarding my affective reaction, it became a turning point in the understanding of the bellicose circumstances around the analysand's superego conflict. In fact, the proceeding analysis demonstrated that her most devastating battlefield was not related to her past or present object relations as such, but to an inner enemy, the archaic superego that was sometimes represented by a crowd of dangerous criminals, sometimes by a murderer disguised as a kind, ordinary man. It was exciting to observe how the most primitive drive instinctual urges as well as her longing for revenge had become internalized, as fiercely amplified, into the superego. In the course of the proceeding analysis the disconnected superego elements became consolidated around the father of the primal scene and his wrath. As a child, she had been frightened to death of her voyeuristic urge becoming detected by her father. Also her sadomasochistic excitement, the spell, became understood in the context of the structural conflict. Her Witches' Sabbath reflected not only the ego's struggle for psychic survival, but it also signified eternal punishment for forbidden sexual acts, damnation.

During the last year of analysis Mrs. D got in touch with her feminine identification and authentic womanliness. This change was related to the final reconstruction of the Oedipus complex in the transference and its painful dissolution.

The maid of the family, a fresh and natural young woman, who had been caring for the analysand from the age of 5, had played a central role at the outbreak of her neurotic conflict. The maid had left the house after having become pregnant and getting married, when the analysand was 11 years old. In leaving, the maid had been very sad, which Mrs. D had interpreted as a sign of punishment for the sexual crime. This incident proved to be fatal for the girl's feminine identification. It opened gates to regression that we already know about.

Why did this incident have such dramatic consequences? At the unconscious level, the maid leaving the house was experienced by the analysand as the banishment for incestuous wishes. It had signified for her a replica of her own experience of being sent to the hospital in the middle of her oedipal phase. As the analysis came to a conclusion, it was perfectly clear that the nucleus of the capsule was formed by the father turning his face away from his daughter, thus signifying her love to be worthless.

Mrs. D's ego ideal had not been irreversibly injured, which made her analysis possible. In proceeding with our work, the ego ideal became represented by the love of her youth. This man extensively dealt with throughout the analysis, had meant for her an ideal of integrity and discretion. With him, she thought, she would have been able to live as a whole person, and thus to experience sexual satisfaction. Only after working through the painful disillusionment, not only in this relationship, but in her analytical relationship as well, could she realize that the loss of an unattainable love does not signify losing human dignity.

Finally, we could also reconstruct the original breach in her psychic foundation. When she had experienced herself to be ultimately abandoned during the last days in the hospital, her violent and justified fury had become abruptly silenced. Since then, the integrated affect of anger had been replaced by cruelty and the willingness to compromise in perceiving reality, which she also understood to lie beyond her tendency to act out.

On the Ego Integrity

Herulf (1991) deals with the concept of integrity as follows:

> I want to stress that the concept is gestalt, a whole, which is more than a sum of the listed parts. One of the most important parts is *wholeness*. A person who has integrity *feels whole and is also regarded as a whole person by others*, which has to do with an inner cohesiveness based on a stabilized inner integration and a satisfying sense of identity and firmness plus a neutral ability *to preserve the boundaries inward and outward*. . . .
>
> Integrity also contains *the understanding of the brokenness, finiteness and the inherent chaos of man, his life and his world—but also of his dignity* [p. 92].

Herulf derives integrity from two sources, namely, the instinct of self-preservation and a phylogenetically determined shape described, for instance, by Gaddini (1982), Green (1986), and myself (Salonen, 1989). He outlines a sequence of psychic integrations, which then culminates in genital narcissistic integrity. Achieving this level of integration presupposes a painful acceptance of the reality principle, which not only means the surrender of infantile pleasures, but the establishment of a new capability as well: inner reflection.

What is said above is closely related to ego autonomy which comprises a crucial psychic development. Ego autonomy is based on the drive instinctual urges being dealt with at the inner level within a frame that is originally placed at the ego's disposal through primary identification. As a matter of fact, ego autonomy is based upon the complex system of psychic regulation that we call conscience in everyday language. Therefore, a more extensive analysis of this system is needed to understand our topic.

In his *Inhibitions, Symptoms and Anxiety*, Freud (1926) outlines the conscience as a major system of psychic regulation. According to him, this regulation consists of a polarity between two faculties, one of them being the signal anxiety at the ego's disposal, the other being the avoidance of traumatic helplessness at the basic level of psychic function. After the establishment of the superego structure, the ego will be furnished with an efficient instrument to control traumatic helplessness. By sending a signal of anxiety, it is capable of summoning the pleasure principle at the basic level, which then leads to defensive measures on a large scale to maintain the psychic equilibrium.

The early frame of primary identification plays a central role in anchoring the conscience to the pleasure principle as well as to the avoidance of traumatic helplessness. The urge for psychic survival is related to this frame as well as the capacity for psychic representation. There is a sound basis for thinking that this configuration constitutes the early foundation of the ego ideal, the main vehicle of the pleasure principle in advanced psychic organization.

The other anchorage of the conscience consists in signal anxiety. It comes into existence after the superego has been established. This signal is the ego's principle tool in maintaining its autonomy. Because signal anxiety is relatively weak and feeble, in comparison to the instinctual forces it commands, it forms a vulnerable point of psychic regulation. On the other hand, the ego is tempted, under pressure of drive instinctual urges, to disregard the signal representing the reality principle. In fact, everyday psychoanalytic experience demonstrates how frail, and how prone to regression this regulation system is.

Rangell (1974) places man's integrity at the center of psychoanalytic interest. In analyzing the compromise of integrity in politics as well as within the psychoanalytic movement, he compares it to neurosis in an interesting way. According to him, instinctual pressures are to neuroses as ego interests are to the compromise of integrity (Rangell, 1974). The perception of reality can be easily deluded by various interests that attract the ego far more than facing, for instance, the danger of castration. The compromise of integrity and the ego split thus belong together.

Mrs. D's case sheds light on two vulnerable points of ego integrity, the first of which is the traumatic paralysis of the ego ideal, her early hospitalizations, and the other being the ego split in facing the primal scene and genital reality in general. In evaluating their relative importance, I am inclined to think that in her case the ego split was of primary importance. Her "original lie" was indicative of the compromise of integrity. It was then supported by her ego interest of making a fortune.

In the face of castration, her ego had resorted to a fetishistic solution in the form of anal phallicism. Even more regressive modes of defense found expression around her psychosomatic symptoms. Actually, the most archaic aspects of her addictive suffering were related to the fusion with her early mother, and her humiliation. An indicator of this might be that we had to make a considerable effort in analyzing a sadomasochistic scene related to the mother's first marriage, before the genuine primal scene could finally be reconstructed in the transference.

The analysis was characterized by a constant tension between two modes of dealing with the instinctual drive conflicts. On the one hand, there was the psychoanalytic frame, aiming at their psychic representation and a sound perception of reality. On the other hand, there was her compelling need to act out these conflicts, and her ego split in order to avoid facing reality. During her analysis, she was, finally, able to face the instinctual dangers related to genital reality without losing her dignity.

I would like to return to Mrs. D's somatic affections which reflected the failure of her psychic economy. In her being unable to represent her violent affects psychically, they had been resomatized with extremely threatening consequences. Perhaps my own affective reaction signified a turning point toward experiencing integrated affects and dealing with them at the psychic level within the analytical setting.

On Man's Atrocities

The problem of dignity cannot be detached from its dark shadow; man's atrocities indicate the precariousness of the structural achievements described before. This shadow has been extensively discussed within psychoanalysis, when solutions have been sought for the humiliation, shame, and guilt that is felt, especially after the Holocaust and the Nazi regime. The thirty-fourth International Psychoanalytic Congress, Hamburg, 1985, was dedicated to this topic. This occasion has been perhaps the most important attempt, up to the present time, to examine psychoanalytically this inconceivable collapse of human dignity. With the thought that much psychoanalytic understanding can still be derived from this disaster, I have included Lifton's (1986) study on the Nazi doctors in my source material, despite the fact that it is not based on psychoanalytic experience. This material not only visualizes the extreme humiliation to which the victims were exposed, but also the compromise of integrity, which formed the background to these deeds.

It is bewildering to realize how few of the leading German doctors actually resisted the establishment of the treatment institutions for mentally retarded and chronically ill children, institutions, which, in fact, formed the experimental field for the future arrangements on a large scale, the concentration camps. Eugenics formed an intermediary science, offering to the doctors a conceptual bridge from the health of the individual to the "health" of the mythic *Volk*. In following the scientific rules scrupulously, the doctors were able to transfer the principles of hygiene into a new, delusional context. In fact, they permitted their conscience and ethical values to be compromised in preferring their conventional ego interests to a simple perception of reality (e.g., their career or scientific interests). According to Lifton, also the doctors' scientific idealism contributed to this compromise of integrity. What made them criminals were, however, their actual deeds, transgressing the frame of human dignity.

There are good grounds for thinking that the concentration camps represented a delusional frame which formed the core of the Nazi ideology. They were an embodiment of delusive grandeur, aiming at the elimination of humiliation, shame, and guilt, attributes that characterize man's inner conflict. Those who were thought to remind us of this conflict and concomitantly authentic ego autonomy were to be enslaved or exterminated.

Lifton emphasizes the initiation ceremony of young doctors upon the arrival at the concentration camps, which must have been an extremely shocking experience for them, irrespective of their preliminary ideological training. A new arrival was obliged to take part, together with a senior colleague, in the selections of prisoners at the platform, after they disembarked from the train. The doctor had to decide, on quasimedical grounds, which of the prisoners were to be taken into forced labor and which were to be sent immediately to the gas chambers. This *actual deed* of selection was the irreversible step in the corruption of the doctor's value system and psychic function. In the midst of extreme psychic trauma, this act, often combined with heavy drinking, signified the identification with a senior colleague and with the delusional frame that he represented. What took place is comparable to the primary identification, this time on delusional grounds. The traumatically shattered ego ideal thus became replaced by the Nazi ideology, forming no frame for psychic elaboration of drive instinctual urges, but an ideal for acting them out with disastrous consequences. In interviewing the Nazi doctors some thirty-five years later, Lifton could not find any real change or remorse. At a deeper level, many of them were still adhering to the delusional frame.

Man's atrocities can be seen as an ultimate attempt at intrapsychic adaptation. Tuovinen (1973) examines crime from this point of view. He arrives at the conclusion that a murder, for example, forms a safeguard against a malignant collapse of psychic function. The offender may actually experience dramatic relief after the deed. What follows then is worth noticing. After initially struggling with guilt, a freezing takes place in the offender's inner world, and he is no longer able to deal with his guilt at the psychic level. After analyzing real incidents of incest, filicide, and parricide, Tuovinen makes an important observation. They are desolate deeds without genuine psychic elaboration: "the oedipal drama as an outer real event is acted out in a compelled, impersonal, and loveless form, which is not typical of inner drama. As an inner drama, it is a tragedy, too, but not necessarily a dreary and cold tragedy" (p. 58). This is consistent with my own observations on the role of psychic representation as the carrier of the experience of being alive.

Because the entire psychic organization has been built, to a large extent, on the metaphorical elaboration of instinctual

drives, a breach in the ego ideal may have drastic consequences throughout the psychic organization. Regarding especially the superego conflict, guilt cannot then be dealt with
at the metaphorical level either. After being left at the mercy
of the ruthless law of Talion, the ego may turn into an execu-
tor of the crude id ideas conveyed by the archaic superego.
This is what happens in the case of malignant depression.

A traumatic dissolution of the ego ideal would also explain
man's atrocities in extreme circumstances. What then takes
place is not a pure regression of the superego, but a failure
of the ego ideal, which invalidates the entire psychic regulation with fatal consequences. I agree with Green (personal
communication, April 17, 1991) that man's atrocities not only
derive from a regression to infantile modes of psychic function. They also derive from the adult ego dealing with traumatic helplessness when the frame for an inner solution is no
longer available.

In concluding my study, I will return to the message that
my patient's mother sent to her daughter's analyst: A woman
who has lost three of her children to death cannot bring up
a child in a better way. In forming a turning point in the analysis, this incident was indicative of the mother's integrity in the
face of her own death. She had been able to deal psychically
with her traumatic past, and to accept, without unbearable
feelings of guilt, her imperfection as a mother. I think that
we have returned to Bertolucci's film; the servants carrying
an urn in their hands with dignity.

References

Chasseguet-Smirgel, J. (1985a), *Creativity and Perversion.* London: Free
    Association Books.
——— (1985b), *The Ego Ideal.* London: Free Association Books.
——— (1992), Some thoughts on the psychoanalytic situation. *J. Amer.
    Psychoanal. Assn.*, 40:3–26.
Freud, S. (1926), Inhibitions, symptoms and anxiety. *Standard Edition*,
    20:75–172. London: Hogarth Press, 1959.

Gaddini, E. (1982), Early defensive fantasies and the psychoanalytical process. *Internat. J. Psycho- Anal.*, 63:379–388.

Green, A. (1986), *On Private Madness.* London: Hogarth Press/Institute of Psycho-Analysis.

Herulf, B. (1991), The integrity of the psychoanalyst. *Scand. Psychoanal. Rev.*, 14:91–105.

Klein, H., & Kogan, I. (1986), Identification process and denial in the shadow of Nazism. *Internat. J. Psycho-Anal.*, 67:45–52.

Lifton, R. J. (1986), *Medical Killing and the Psychology of Genocide.* London: Macmillan.

McDougall, J. (1989), *Theaters of Body: A Psychoanalytical Approach to Psychosomatic Illness,* New York and London: W. W. Norton.

Rangell, L. (1974), A psychoanalytic perspective leading currently to the syndrome of the compromise of integrity. *Internat. J. Psycho-Anal.*, 55:3–12.

Salonen, S. (1989), The restitution of primary identification in psychoanalysis. *Scand. Psychoanal. Rev.*, 12:102–115.

——— (1992), The reconstruction of psychic trauma. *Scand. Psychoanal. Rev.*, 15:89–103.

Tuovinen, M. (1973), *Crime as an Attempt at Intrapsychic Adaptation.* Acta Universitatis Ouluensis, Series D, Medica No. 2, Psychiatrica No. 1. University of Oulu, Oulu.

4

The Intersubjective Constitution of the Sense of Disappearing in Schizophrenia: A Phenomenological Description of a Healthy Sibling's Intuitions

Maurice Apprey, Ph.D.

> For with my own eyes I myself saw Sibyl sitting in a cage at Cumae, and when the boys asked her: "Sibyl, what do you want?" She answered: "I want to die."
> Petronius Arbiter

> To know death better is to put it back in its rightful place.
> Louis-Vincent Thomas

In 1986 James Grotstein made astute observations in a phenomenological account of schizophrenia. In discussing contributions by psychoanalytic and other researchers on family theories of schizophrenia (R. W. Lidz and T. Lidz, 1949;

Jackson, Block, and Peterson, 1958; Wynne, Ryckoff, Day and Hirsch, 1958; Jackson and Weakland, 1959; Bowen, 1960; Lidz, Fleck, and Cornelison, 1965; T. Lidz, 1973; Wynne, Singer and Bartko, 1975), he observed that the phenomenal world of the schizophrenic is fraught with feelings of vagueness and unreality, perceived threat of the schizophrenic's disappearance, and sacrificial ostracization. Building on his prior work, Grotstein (1983) observed that this predator anxiety, with the attendant feeling of being unprotected, is based on the experience of being chosen to be sacrificed to predators. He suggested that "there is a proliferation of predator anxiety in the delusional and hallucinatory phenomenology of these patients" (Grotstein, 1986), and that:

> The predator imagery is not just the transformation of instinctual impulses, but seems to be the inescapable imagery that devolves when infants, or even adults, believe themselves to be abandoned by their loved objects and therefore to be the inescapable victims of the inevitable predators that are always believed to be just outside the protection of the family or group [pp. 40–41].

In the dream world of these schizophrenics, Grotstein (1986) noted many reports of "eerie experiences and/or dreams in which they believed they had died, that is, they seemed to have become mysteriously changed by and engulfed into terror" (p. 41). However, after the experience of change, the schizophrenic knew of that experience but no one else knew of the transformation into, let us say, an "abstract world of randomness" (p. 41), or of being enclosed in an invisible capsule. Grotstein (1986) went further to link the experience of transformation into death to the work of researchers on family theories of schizophrenia in the following way:

> The exclusive family hypotheses would suggest that the future schizophrenic is selected as the "human sacrifice" by the family system and becomes quickly "notarized" by siblings and

peer groups. Involved in this choice of sacrifice is the group process in which there is a projective identification of the shortcomings of each of the members, and of the group compositely, into the one chosen for sacrifice so as to rid the group and its members of the taint of defectiveness [p. 61].

Descriptive psychoanalytic observations, such as those by Grotstein and other clinical researchers are abbreviated and often determined within the bounds of the particular school of thought. The result is that there is the imprint of drive theory, ego psychology, psychoanalytic self psychology, and one or more object relations theories. However, the potential for premature closure in terms of our psychoanalytic findings is always there precisely because theories confine us to what they are able to describe.

Suppose, then, that we wished to conduct a more open-ended and yet equally rigorous study with a disciplined phenomenological praxis inspired by the philosophy of Edmund Husserl but grounded in a phenomenological psychological praxis (see Giorgi, 1979, 1985). We would be in a better position to unpack the phenomena Grotstein and others have observed in psychoanalytic research on schizophrenia.

Phenomenology

Before unpacking some of the findings in psychoanalytic research, we must have a working knowledge of what phenomenology is. Graumann (1988) defined the term *phenomenological* the following way: It is "Not a label for a philosophical school or a psychological metatheory or even theory, but a methodological attitude for looking at problems in the human sciences, for reflecting on them, and for asking questions accordingly" (p. 35). Because it is a problem-centered attitude, Graumann (1988) sees phenomenology, then, "not as a fixture, and hence not codified in the sense of a methodological canon. Its openness is both its strength and its weakness" (p. 35).

To correct the potential weakness in the openness of phenomenology, Giorgi (1979) outlined a praxis for conducting phenomenological psychological research.

Phenomenological Praxis

Briefly described, Giorgi's (1979) method is as follows:

1. The researcher reads the entire description of the [phenomenon] straight through to get a sense of the whole.

2. Next, the researcher reads the same description more slowly and delineates each time that a transition in meaning is perceived with respect to the intention of discovering the meaning of [the phenomena]. After this procedure he has a series of meaning units or constituents.

3. The researcher then eliminates redundancies and clarifies or elaborates . . . the meaning of the units . . . just constituted by relating them to each other and to the sense of the whole.

4. The researcher reflects on the given units, still expressed essentially in the concrete language of the subject, and comes up with the essence of that situation for the subject with respect to the phenomenon [under study]. Each unit is systematically interrogated for what it reveals about the phenomenon in that situation for that subject. The researcher transforms each unit, when relevant, into the language of psychological science.

5. "The researcher synthesizes and integrates the insights achieved into a consistent description of the structure" [of experience of that phenomenon under study] (p. 83).

In 1985 Giorgi combined steps 3 and 4 which constitute the abstraction of essences from the subject's naive descriptions. Naive descriptions are the researcher's verbatim transcripts, uncontaminated by theory or the interpretations of a researcher. In the phenomenological psychological praxis "naive" means that the researcher has not as yet conducted the eidetic abstractions (steps 3 and 4) which would collapse together to determine the intersubjective structure of experience.

The intersubjective dimension of phenomenology was captured in the description by the French philosopher, Merleau-Ponty (1962).

Working Definition of Phenomenology

Merleau-Ponty (1962) thus defined phenomenology:

> Phenomenology is the study of essences, and according to it, all problems amount to finding definitions of essences: the essence of perception, or the essence of consciousness, for example. But phenomenology is also a philosophy which puts essences back into existence, and does not expect to arrive at an understanding of man and the world from any starting point other than that of their "facticity" [p. vii].

The intersubjective and the circular element of putting essences back into existence requires that the phenomenological researcher account for his or her findings by ensuring that the reader would see how the set of results, that is, the intersubjective structure of experience was determined. In this approach, even if the reader does not agree with the results, he or she must nevertheless follow how the results were arrived at. Thus the reader is free to determine another perspective of the same phenomenon under study.

Let us now embark on the study that would provide us with an intersubjective constitution of the sense of disappearing, that of being sacrificed in schizophrenia, that Grotstein and the family theorists have observed.

Context of Phenomenological Study

Prior studies (Apprey and Stein, 1993) have provided me with various accounts in anorexia nervosa and transsexualism, of the sense of disappearing or of being sacrificed. This phenomenon has been noted in schizophrenia by Grotstein. I was, therefore, most curious to know how that sense of disappearance shows itself in schizophrenia.

For a study of this phenomenon of disappearance I interviewed a family member, one subject, and conducted a phenomenological study on her audiotaped and verbatim account of how she sees her schizophrenic brother. This volunteer subject indicated that her mother was on her way to abort her when in the middle of the journey she decided to carry her to full term, and she was curious to know how her brother was connected to their mother. She hoped to contribute and to learn.

Intuitions from a schizophrenic sibling's phenomenal world are important data within the broader phenomenological psychological tradition, because for phenomenologists every perception is given in a profile with potential for rich details. In the words of Roman Ingarden (1975), a student of Husserl:

> Every particular outer perception (e.g., seeing) is in its essence "partial" (in parts) and not adequate to what is given in it. It is one-sided and partial apprehension of the perceived object and the "other side"—which is turned away from the perceiving subject—and the interior of the thing is only co-given or co-meant. . . . Only in the further course of the experience (encounter), i. e., in other perceptions of "the same" thing can the back become the front and then it is given effectively, explicitly. . . . These later perceptions of the same thing can corroborate the result of the actual perception but that is not necessary [p. 14].

The subject's intuitions of her brother's illness and its place in her family will, therefore, be encountered, first by her, as a lived experience, then by the researcher who engages the same material, and then by reference to other works by the author who has written about other phenomena that may be in the same horizon but need not be interchangeable.

Let us now bracket (i.e., suspend) our knowledge of schizophrenia and enter the world of a subject whose brother is a schizophrenic with only one question: "Describe for me in a very concrete way how you see your brother." Any further questions from the research must only be based on the utterances of the subject and for the purpose of clarification. There were twelve interviews in all. For this paper only the analysis of the data from the first interview will be shown.

Conducting the Phenomenological Study

For the sake of efficiency and confidentiality, I shall select the relevant naive descriptions (step 1), that have been separated out into meaning units (step 2) and show the eidetic abstractions of units 1–88 (i.e., the determination of essences in step 3). I shall then indicate the results of the study of the experience of disappearing in the schizophrenic (in step 4), which is the structure of experience.

Phenomenological Presence

Before the analysis of the data, I shall disclose the phenomenological presence that I bring to this study. Preconceptions, concepts, theories, experiences that inform my phenomenological presence have had to be suspended, according to Husserl's concept of epoche, that is, bracketed, in order not to prejudice the results of the study.

A part of my phenomenological presence is experiential; another part is theoretical. Experientially, this paper was very difficult for me to write. At a conference in Cancun, Mexico, two years ago, James Grotstein asked me if I had any interest in writing about schizophrenia. I answered "No" before I could think about his question. Since then my precipitous answer has troubled me. How could I say "No" after having worked with schizophrenics in multiple settings in three countries? A year later Vamık Volkan asked me the same question, but this time my answer was much less precipitous. I was now only willing to consider writing about schizophrenia. Nevertheless I had received both questions as if I had experienced them as violence on schizophrenics if I wrote about them. At the very conclusion of the writing of this chapter "I woke up." My resistance to writing was based on the unconscious assumption that schizophrenics are to be taken care of, not written about. It was as though one could not both write about them and treat them.

The theoretical part of my phenomenological presence is as follows. It has always intrigued me that Franz Brentano, a Catholic priest, who was a philosopher and mathematician, taught both Freud and Husserl philosophy, and yet the latter went in the direction of pure description and the former in the direction of interpretation. Husserl and Freud were born about the same year and died within one year of each other. Both Freud and Husserl were influenced by Brentano's key notions of intentionality, perceptual content, containment, dependence, aggregate, proper part, integral whole, and so on. Brentano anteceded Bion's elaboration of "container-contained." Not easily influenced by dichotomies, I have sought to find ways to bring together description and interpretation. This is my lifelong project. It is for this reason that I begin a research inquiry with descriptive praxes and then subsequently try to potentiate my findings with interpretation. In this way I follow Bachelard (1969) and Merleau-Ponty (1962) in making complementarities out of antinomies.

Phenomenological Praxis

Steps 1 (Naive Descriptions) and 2 (Selected Meaning Units)

1. My fantasy about my brother, is I don't know if it meets with reality but, I think that he and I are two different things to my mother because I don't have any hard information

about this. For what I see, my brother represents something very important to my mother that links her with my father who died three months before I was born.

2. My brother was 2½ when my father died. Apparently the story goes that my father and he were very close and that he worshipped my brother, and he also worshipped the idea of having a little girl, that I was kind of what the doctor ordered for him but whom he did not get to see.

6. My brother represents some link or hold that my mother has to my father who she apparently, although she doesn't talk about this very much, and only recently has shared some things with me about this on asking her, loved him very dearly.

9. My father became very ill from working with radar equipment in the Army and got leukemia very suddenly and died only three weeks after he was diagnosed. Apparently he had black and blue marks that showed up on his body, and they checked him out, and he had a cerebral hemorrhage while my mother was home with him. He went blind and said to my mother that he couldn't see and my mother didn't take it seriously.

10. She didn't take him to the hospital right away. That is what she doesn't talk about very much.

11. Subsequently he died that day when he went off, not with her, to the hospital, after I guess, they realized how serious it was. And she has just suppressed it ever since. She has never talked about it, I don't think, with anybody except for me very recently, and my brother has been her project.

12. Well, and this is where I am guessing that it has some link to, has to do with my father, my mother's whole life has been involved in making my brother a doctor. . . .

13. He is very brilliant. He tests up in the genius range in intelligence. . . . He did exceptionally well at school and my mother went out of her way to prepare him for that with the best private schools.

14. In the summer while other kids were playing, my brother was studying, and was very much a bookworm, and did not have many friends.

16. She still cooks for him, she cleans for him, she shops for his clothes, she has kept him at home like a little boy who has never had an opportunity to grow up.

19. [After being kicked out of a major U.S. medical school his mother enrolled him in a medical school in a Spanish-speaking country] and he had to learn Spanish. He taught himself seven other languages. Apparently it wasn't hard for him to pick up a book and teach himself a new language. In his spare time growing up, while other kids were playing, he was rewriting Einstein's theory the way he thought it should be.

20. And so my mother has always been very bonded and proud of my brother and linked with my brother in a very special way . . . almost where there is something too close about that for comfort . . . and not incestuous in any way . . . she has never been inappropriate in that way, not behaviorally, but in a sense, my mother has never had a successful relationship with a man and so in a way maybe there is an incestuous component. It's almost like she is married to her little man.

21. Her current marriage is built around my stepfather helping my mother with my brother, and that is the only reason she stays with him. She uses him because he takes care of, watches my brother, and she is afraid that she couldn't handle the whole situation alone.

22. It gets real complicated because she has had an affair with a man for six years while she uses my stepfather to baby-sit my brother. There is a real sickness in all this. My stepfather's whole meaning now is built around babying my brother and basically diapering him.

23. An example I could give is one morning we went out for breakfast about a year ago and my stepfather was gloating

about how if he didn't feed my brother, didn't cook for him, and make his meals, he didn't know how he would survive. . . .

24. And my mother has the same fear that if she wasn't there for him . . . he would die.

26. So what they do is spend exorbitant amounts of money on psychiatry and basically a medical degree, because he is a doctor but he didn't make it through what they call the fifth pathway at the very end when he was done. He wasn't allowed to practice because he had another mental breakdown and so he is basically disabled, crippled mentally, I feel, from his belief that he would die if they weren't there to take care of him. He has bought into that belief so much that he is terrified to be out of my mother's clutches. I call them clutches because she is a very forceful, overbearing, Jewish mother who loves her son.

32. The new thing that my mother shared with me is that he chokes now when she talks to him about the idea of driving. Because of the lights he panics and then he starts to choke and claims that he can't breathe. . . .

35. She either loves him or hates him and there doesn't seem to be any middle ground.

36. [When she loves him] she buys him expensive sweaters, which he can't afford to buy, this is a cultural thing. She drives him to the doctor . . . to every doctor on earth to try to fix him. . . . She is convinced that it's because he went to "x" college for his undergraduate work that he did drugs and that ruined him. She is always looking for an external reason to explain this and she really doesn't, even deep in her heart, she doesn't believe that he has an illness. I think she thinks somebody else did this to him because she said to me this week on the phone, "If I had just not sent him to 'x' college none of this would have happened."

37. And what she wants me to do now, the most recent thing . . . is asking me to call psychiatrists and ask them to help

because nobody else is helping. In trying to get him to come visit me, to be a good sister, and be more available to him, she wants me to call him and . . .

38. and this is where I am bordering into the hatred part now. She runs away from him every weekend.

40. Rather than help me with my schooling, all of [her] money has gone to my brother and [visits to] Paris and a second house in "y" state and a Cadillac and her clothing, and a face-lift—two face-lifts,

41. and one of them was on the day that my son was having a circumcision ritual which was a very painful day for me to watch this.

49. She has part relationships with people. She doesn't have a whole relationship with anyone. And even my brother, I think, I mean that just seems to be the focus of everything. My mother somehow needs him to be ill for some reason and I don't know whether. . . . My more recent thoughts about this is that it is some link to my dead father. That to some extent this is an extension of my father's ghost. That she took him on as her man and is trying to make him the man that she has never had, and she has failed, because look what happened to him. He has not become the man.

50. And here is the interesting thing that I have worked hard and responsibly and carried three jobs at a time to become a doctor and she never takes notice of that at all, and I haven't gotten much help. . . . I realize now the whole reason. . . . I even thought it was just for professional reasons that I was becoming a doctor, but that I thought that she would love me like she loved my brother and also make her happy. . . .

51. The reason she had kept me alive is that she hoped that I would bring her hope someday. So I think there is some unconscious hope for happiness in her life that I would be. . . .

52. She thought on the way to the abortion clinic that maybe she shouldn't abort me because maybe I would bring her hope and that is all she said. . . .

54. She had always been there for my brother and um I didn't tell her this because she can't listen when I talk to her on the phone. I brought this to her . . . a letter I wanted to write for a long time and had thrown away many times, and I told her that we weren't really very different, that she had goals to be something in her life that her mother thwarted. She wanted to finish college and her mother didn't think she should be like two cousins of hers. They, you know, fit the typical female role in a Jewish family and she never met that goal which may have been her attempt through my brother to finish that piece for herself.

59. Well, I cried a lot especially that day [of the circumcision] because I had her two cousins that she hated by my side and they were the ones who sat there and held my hands in the kitchen because I wouldn't watch the circumcision and um . . . with my aunt, my mother's sister who has kind of been the good perfect child who did what my grandmother wanted. My mother had a mind of her own . . . um . . . and . . . that is what might have gotten to my mother recently . . . is when in a letter I wrote, I just want you to know that I really would have much preferred having you there with me than your two cousins whom you hate. I said and I think that both, I may have done that to hurt her somehow to say, because I knew that would be below the belt line, sore spot just to get her attention to say, "Hey, look here, I wanted you there. I didn't want your two cousins," and maybe that is what got her to listen to me for the first time but as best she can.

61. He screamed. I will never forget it. Just the blood curdling scream and they all say that they hear that it would be seconds and I just can't believe that he wasn't in terrible agony, and all they do is put a little bit of wine on his tongue to anesthetize him a little bit. But he screamed that whole day. I have pictures of his little face from that whole day and anytime you looked at him he looked really very unsettled and all day we had to take him in the car and he would cry with

every move that you made in the car so he must have been in terrible pain and. . . .

62. He [my son] has always been a very demanding child but I think part of what I have done is try to meet every urge . . . um . . . he is temperamental. He cries if he doesn't get what he wants.

63. [What he wants is for me] to play with him. To wait on him. To get him toys. See, I think I spent the first few years going overboard a little bit to make up for what I lost. I didn't ever make him wait for hugs or being picked up, and so I consciously have been jumping to his cries ever since he was born.

66. Lately, he has been a little better, as I have been setting better limits with him, and I have been realizing that I am not a bad mommy like my mother seemed to me, and that I am also very afraid, coming back to my brother, of doing the same thing that my mother did to my brother like overprotecting him and creating wishy-washiness about him, and [so he] wouldn't be able to stand up.

67. My son also seems to have a kind of brilliance of some kind. He is exceedingly smart and it is a little scary. There have been times, as when he was one year old, and he started to fold corners of napkins and make them match up to the corners. . . . He figures things out just like that.

68. But there is a seriousness about him. He doesn't seem as happy-go-lucky as I would like him to be. . . .

70. But I worry. I worry, when he gets demanding and temperamental sometimes, if he has got this seed of the schizophrenia somewhere in him. It is irrational that I am worrying, but I worry. . . if there is something psychologically wrong with him. . . . The demand is not irrational but my belief is irrational that I think that he would become schizophrenic because he has always been demanding. It is interesting that my brother is demanding. He . . . demands that, with me lately, he demands me to buy things for his kids when he can't, and it seems that he is somehow entitled

that we should be doing this for his kids but we just can't. He has two children.

71. [He has two children] from his Spanish wife that he married when he was in——and he was almost killed by them [her family] because he was American and they didn't want her to marry him, and since he was near to crazy, his illness was manifesting itself and he did some crazy things in—— that it is hard to believe he survived.

79. My grandfather, who is also my paternal grandfather, who they think might have been undiagnosed as manic depressive his whole life was . . . and my father's only living brother is. . . . he is homosexual and the family outcast out [on the West coast]. . . .

80. And he wrote a letter to me because I took a family inheritance that he believed was his from his father. When he died he [grandfather] gave me some money. He wrote me a letter that I was going to the Devil and it sounded like a very strange letter like almost he might have been in a psychotic episode.

81. Same theme here about the men on my father's side of the family. His father sat like a recluse and hermit in a chair in his room from 50 to 86 when he died. He retired early for some reason . . . couldn't function outside the home or would walk around the streets of the Bronx with a cane out like this so that nobody would hurt him. I saw him one time walking like that and, um, that's what scares me about my son that there is some theme here, something that has gone on with the men that is going to be passed on to him whenever I see him acting out. I think that it is normal kid stuff that I put my own fears into, and that I am learning how not to do that, and it's getting better and more hopeful than [used to be the case].

83. He sits every evening . . . he doesn't like television very much. He'd much rather be creating and he builds blocks about every night. He builds structures that are beautiful and are very advanced for a little child, and his pictures. His drawings are advanced. . . .

84. Which I hope maybe he got a little bit of that from me because I have a little bit of artistic talent that my uncle . . . my dad's brother is a very talented artist, but, um, he plays well, he creates his own action in acting out. You know, there is another side of him than just this demanding side that, you know. . . .

88. and there was a problem with my brother. My brother came to live with my grandfather, who would give him the shirt off his back, the last few months of my grandfather's life, and he practically destroyed my grandfather. I think that is why he died because my brother had another schizophrenic breakdown and was abusing my grandfather and even pushed him down on the floor which is not like my brother—gentle and passive, head down and shuffles his feet.

Step 3: Eidetic Abstractions (From meaning units of step 2 and from naive descriptions of step 1)

1. Subject (S) states clearly that she is a different project from the project that her brother represents to her mother, and she perceives that her brother is a link between mother and the father who died three months before the subject herself was born.

2. S clarifies further that her father died when S's brother was only 2½ years of age and that before he died he worshipped the brother as well as the idea of having a little girl; an idea that did not materialize because he died before "his little girl" was born.

6. S perceives her brother as one who represents for their mother a present link to or hold on their deceased and thus absent father; a father who S perceives as loving the brother dearly.

9. S recalls that her father was killed by exposure to radioactive rays from military equipment which caused him to become blind and caused his health to deteriorate very rapidly, and yet his wife did not seek help promptly.

10. S surmises that her mother's lack of prompt action caused his death, leading to her subsequent feelings of guilt over her inaction, and hence her guilt-ridden silence over the event of his death.

11. S surmises that what death her mother does not speak of gets staged as a project for her mother, and she stages the death of her husband through the drama of her son's incapacitated life which is hers to manage.

12. S surmises further that her mother sacrificed her whole life in order to incapacitate and repair her son's life and in the process of incapacitating and repairing, she relives a life she would not otherwise speak of.

13. S sees that her mother's project of incapacitating and repairing her son by her own hand only partly succeeded when her mother created an intellectual genius out of him.

14. S sees, in the intensity of mother's project of incapacitating and repairing, a creation of intellectual prowess which is at great cost to the son's social development.

16. S elaborates that her mother kept the son from becoming a man when she continued to cook, clean for him, and buy his clothes, even after, and long after she had incapacitated him by babying him.

19. S suggests that a son supports a mother's project of incapacitating and repairing him when he has the genius to rewrite Einstein's theories, and when the son is capable of studying medicine in a foreign language in another country, he fits into, and submits to her crippling design.

20. S perceives the special link of mother and son as a fit that borders on incest, and although incest has never occurred between them, the near-incestuous tie has kept her mother from maturing in a relationship with a man away from her own son.

21. S finds that her mother has so crippled her son's and her own life that she is afraid of raising her little child/man by herself and has married a second husband who devotes his

whole life to the mother's concealed wish to hurt and repair her son.

22. S is disgusted by her observation that her mother has married one man solely to assist her in injuring and repairing her son, and outside of the marriage, mother has a long-standing sexual liaison with another man.

23. S confirms that the husband who now diapers the crippled brother treats the son now as his to rescue from death, and he does so as though it were something to feel triumphant about.

24. S suggests that stepfather and mother have both created a situation in which they can gloat over and triumph over the death of the son which they perceive they can prevent by overgratifying him.

26. S bemoans her mother's complete success in disabling the son who received the medical degree but cannot practice because he had another mental breakdown upon qualifying. S thus confesses to her experience of her loving mother's forceful, overbearing "clutches" out of which an offspring cannot escape.

32. S hears from her mother an account of the son's choking when she talks to him about the very idea of driving a car, and the possibility of lights frightens him.

35. S perceives that her mother either hates or loves her son in categorical terms only.

36. S perceives that her mother shows her love for her son by buying sweaters for him that he cannot afford, going to excessive lengths to find medical experts who can prove that she did not injure her son, and that someone other than she caused her son's schizophrenia. In this sense, S perceives that her mother's sense of love is tied to being blameless for her son's illness.

37. S observes that her mother wants her to participate in the devastation as though a good sister does so.

38. S perceives that when her mother hates her ill son she deserts him, which is what she does every weekend.

40. S elaborates that her mother acts as though if she can change her face with face-lifts and if she can manifest material possessions, her life would be less painful, more humane, and value-laden.

41. S observes that when she was offering her son the rite of circumcision, her mother was offering herself a face-lift rather than coming to spare her the pain of watching circumcision and enduring her pain alone.

49. S surmises further that when mother's partial relationships do not tear her mother away from her ill son, those partial relationships only serve to preserve that dysfunctional tie to her son. In preserving that problem-ridden tie to her son she seeks to both preserve her son, who undergoes damage and repair at her hands, as husband incarnate, a phantom. As phantom her son is neither alive, nor a grown man, and thus she failed to preserve her husband as well as failed to raise her son into becoming a man.

50. S realizes now that she has her own project of desiring to become a holder of a doctoral degree so that her mother would love her like she loves her brother and also, she hopes that in getting a doctoral degree she will make her mother happy. However, S fears that all her efforts to get additional education and to please her mother continues to be secondary to her mother's primary project of creating and preserving her husband's phantom through her immobilized son.

51. S surmises that her mother kept her alive in order to bring her mother hope and happiness for herself.

52. S theorizes that by trying to please her mother, she hooked herself up onto her mother's desire for happiness, and in getting hooked up with her mother's desire, she hoped that her mother would notice that she lives.

54. S sees in her frustrated desire for her mother's love a repeat of her mother's own unmet needs by her mother's mother. However, S perceives that her mother chose her brother as the offspring who must embody and fulfill her wishes for success in life.

59. S protests that it was her mother's two cousins that the mother hates who were there to hold her hand during her son's circumcision while her own mother was absent. Further, S recognizes that one of her mother's sisters was a perfect child who always did what she was told whereas S's mother tried to rebel. In rebelling, S's mother is perceived as being like S whose rebellion took the form of escaping the family's infusion of illness.

61. S agonizes as she recalls "the blood-curdling scream" that came from her son during his circumcision and feels that the circumcision was most hurtful to him.

62. S notices now that the hurt child has turned into a most demanding child who cries to get his needs met and who usually succeeds in getting his mother to meet his demands.

63. S readily meets her son's demands for her to play with him, wait on him, get him toys, give him hugs, and has met his demands from the moment of his birth.

66. S notices that she is making progress in setting limits for her demanding son. In noticing that she is not a bad mother like her own mother was, she is not afraid to offer him the structure that he needs in order not to become like the incapacitated son that her mother created.

67. S notices further her own fear of creating another incapacitated son because she is afraid that her son's precocity, which she sees as brilliance, is akin to her brother's intellectual brilliance.

68. S observes that her son is a serious child.

70. S worries that when her son becomes "demanding and temperamental," there is a risk that the seed of psychosis will be passed on and planted in him.

71. S recalls that in the throes of her brother's psychosis, he was almost killed by his wife-to-be's family who had not wanted him to marry her. He now has two children.

79. S traces the paralysis of her brother's condition to her paternal grandfather who was an undiagnosed manic

depressive, her paternal uncle who is a homosexual, and a family outcast.

80. S is horrified by her paternal uncle's claim that she received money as an inheritance from his father that belongs to him, and for that reason she was going to the Devil; a situation that tells S that her uncle was both homosexual and psychotic.

81. S is petrified that the men on the paternal side of her family could pass on psychological paralysis from one generation to another when she recalls that her paternal grandfather, the undiagnosed manic depressive, was also a recluse for thirty-six years before he died, could not function outside his home, and when he was outside held his walking cane in a way that would ensure that no one touched him.

83. S perceives that her son is advanced for his age which he shows in the models he builds or creates when he is at play.

84. S hopes that her son got some of his creative ability from her and, in part, from her father's artistic brother, but fears the origins and consequences of her son's demandingness.

88. S views her mother's father's generosity as two-sided: he gave selflessly to the family, but the same generosity killed him when he allowed S's paralyzed brother to live with him in a way that colluded with the brother's destruction. In one of his breakdowns the otherwise gentle brother abused his generous grandfather and pushed him onto the floor.

Results: Structure of Experience (step 4 of the praxis)

An offspring who is a present link to an absent and deceased father can be summoned to stage his father's death if the surviving parent can create a situation where the son's incapacitated life can mimic his father's death. The mother as surviving parent, may sacrifice her whole life to ensure the mental paralysis of her son at the same time as she strives to repair the paralysis she engineered. Hence, paralysis of the son is juxtaposed to an attempted repair of his crippled mental life. By creating an intellectual genius of a son a parent can create the semblance of a repair; a feigned repair that is so single-mindedly focused and incapacitating that his social development is severely impoverished. In the same vein of incapacitating a son, a mother may indulge and baby a son no matter what his age is. Such an incapacitating circumstance, however, does not happen without the benefit of a child's own disposition and natural gifts. When a son, therefore, is capable of rewriting Einstein's theories, capable of studying medicine for a potential career in a foreign country, and in a foreign language, he suitably fits into and submits to a mother's design and horizon where becoming an intellectual genius promises a mask of repair. Such a repair of one's own incapacitating actions can, however, be onerous. As such, the job of creating a child-man, a caricature of a man, as it were, in her son is so great that her second husband must be recruited to join in with her project of mental paralysis of a son and the semblance of a repair. In mother's world then, one man may be needed to help paralyze the son whilst a second man, outside of her marriage, may be needed to meet her sexual needs. To the crippling parental figures, it is a triumph to provide supervision for the son's living death and to think that they can overturn his living death by overindulging him. Henceforth death is synonymous with overindulgence in the world of such a supervisory and complicit couple. As if the son's intellectual disposition were not enough to provide a fit for mother's project, the son's proneness to choking when opportunities arise for him to charge off and tear away from his mother, link him to a familial history of choking when a person is anxious. It is as though the son's choking were a transgenerational and familial legacy. For the family the physical sensation of choking to death is a remembered sensation. Henceforth, remembering in sensation is a communal affair. To avert his choking to death, or rather mother's fear of it, the supervisory couple of mother and stepfather create a paradoxical situation where a son's indulgence equals both his demise and an alibi of blamelessness for his paralysis.

There is a motor that drives the push toward a son's paralysis. That motor is a hatred which alternates with excessive demonstrations of love. Hatred and love rapidly change places and there is no room for mixed feelings in this world, so that a parent can create a situation of excessive dependence on a daily basis only to abandon him for the luxury of her second home that is located out of state. In her world it is as though extravagance would provide her with a sense of value and esteem. It is as though face-lifts would change her fate so that her life would become less painful and more humane. For mother then, a face-lift comes first, a grandson's circumcision rite a distant second. In the situation where mother has partial and unconsummated relationships with men she ensures that her project of paralysis and repair is left intact, and in the process, she can create a phantom man, a phantom husband out of her child and a son who is neither fully alive, nor an emotionally grown man.

There are others, besides the mother and stepfather who have a project. The ill brother's sister too has her project which glides past her mother's. When mother overinvests in her son, a daughter too must strive to get back her mother's love. She will strive to become a doctor so that her mother will love her, refusing to recognize that her project does not intersect with her mother's. As to her mother's project for her, she is the daughter who must be aborted and if not aborted, she must live to give hope to a young expectant mother who already has a second child and who has just lost her husband. Striving to hook her own project onto her mother's, a daughter may hope that her mother will notice that she lives, that she survived, that she did not die. Daughter may have one more strategy, which is to teach her mother that both she and her mother were disappointed by their mothers and hence they would do well to cooperate. As if at war with their various projects for one another, mother's project, not of requiring a daughter to become a doctor, but that of requiring her to become a Jewish bubba may be proposed only to be rejected, recognizing as the daughter does that if mother would not accept her mother's wish for her to be a Jewish bubba, she as granddaughter must not be one either. Perhaps a third strategy by the daughter could get her mother's attention, and it is the strategy of demonstrating to her mother that they both survived their mothers' imposition when they appropriately rebeled.

In such a world where some projects intersect or glide past one another, others successfully slip through, and ownership of a project may be passed on or, at least shared. What killing may not be successfully carried out, except through the creating of a son's paralysis, revived in the consideration of abortion, may enter into another parent's style of parenting. The result is that daughter waits till her son is 3 months of age before circumcising him and fears, as a result of his blood curdling scream, that she could have killed him with that hurtful circumcision. To her then, a hurt child must be indulged, and his excessive demands must be met. Afraid, however, that she might create her brother in her son, she recognizes that the way to become different from her mother is to set limits for her son so that he does not become ill like her brother. The similarities between daughter's son and mother's ill son are worrisome to the daughter. They are both brilliant, both very demanding and temperamental, both serious, both indulged. Hence, similarity is an opening for infusion of immobilizing illness, specifically of psychosis. For such a daughter, the infusion of psychosis is real, bearing in mind a deceased manic depressive forebear, a homosexual and psychotic uncle who is also at war with her over an imagined financial legacy that he believes should have gone to him but went to her. If, however, the daughter's son could preserve his artistic skills which he got from her and from her father's brother, and if she could limit his demandingness, she sees hope in her son, a projected future "leader."

Discussion

There is a little known passage in Heinz Hartmann's (1964) work on understanding and explanation in which he discussed, inter alia, Dilthey's line of thought in human sciences. He wrote that "the results of phenomenological psychology are a necessary foundation upon which explanatory psychology builds, and that such results, when they are firmly established, may also be used in psychoanalytic research" (p. 376). He heartily subscribed to Kronfeld's view (1920):

> Phenomenology is a preliminary approach necessary for any psychological theory which seeks to explain phenomena (genetically); it is a preliminary approach in the same sense that any psychological ontology is. It is on the one hand the precondition for the formation of the theories, and on the other hand it demands such theories; otherwise it remains essentially incomplete [p. 394; Hartmann 1964, p. 376].

These comments would suggest that descriptions must precede interpretation and that description and interpretation can be continuous. It is the sequence of description and interpretation that promises to provide us with more complete results.

In the above study on the intersubjective constitution of the sense of disappearance in schizophrenia, we have determined at least five elements that constitute our results. Unpacking the schizophrenic experience of disappearing in the systematic phenomenological study, a sequence of experiences shows itself in a provisional intersubjective constitution as follows:

1. An injunction to die is established;
2. A summons to submit to the injunction is rendered;
3. An anterior (m)other seeks a constitutional or environmental fit to make the project of nonexistence feasible;

4. The chosen subject submits;

5. A complicit project of subject adhering to the deadly injunction and an attendant but feigned attempt to repair the damage follows. (Compromise, from Latin "Compromittere" which means "to make a shared promise," is perhaps a better and deeper meaning of this element.)

The schizophrenic experience of disappearing is, therefore, a composite set of imperatives that constitute an aporia, a dead-end that houses an anterior parent's preoccupation with death.

There is no implication here of the concept of the schizophrenogenic mother. In other studies I put forward the notion of apposition, that is, placing parents in a transgenerational context, to avoid such an easy temptation of blaming mothers (Apprey and Stein, 1993). There is an implication here, however, for the psychoanalytic treatment of the schizophrenic. I shall only comment on the implications for handling the transference at this stage of the study. If there is an imperative to die it will show itself in the transference. When it shows itself in the transference, it might be helpful to see the transference as a two-pronged experience in which the analyst is urgently invited to collude in the sacrifice of the analysand. At the same time the analyst has the opportunity to form an alliance with the analysand for the purpose of overturning the received injunction to die. Thus the analysand gradually comes to see that the person of the analyst in the transference stands for his emancipation as opposed to the feigned repair imposed by the anterior (m)other to serve the purposes of self-deception and preservation of the death sentence.

Two examples of the use of the analyst to serve the purpose of the analysand's emancipation can be found in Volkan (1995). In the case of Jane, her father, whose mother was psychotic when he was growing up, constituted the world as a dangerous place where a mother is perceived as a woman who gives birth to a child and imperils its life. Hence, Jane, the baby girl must be sacrificed. In the case of Attis, the preservation of his death sentence takes the symbolic form of an older brother cutting off his finger, which the mother preserves in a jar with the hope that it could be mentally or physically sutured back to his hand. Volkan's careful observations and his handling of the transference in both cases give us cause to rethink how we describe the work of treating schizophrenic patients psychoanalytically. Through careful observations, clinical or phenomenological, we may come to see more clearly what peremptory summons are conveyed in psychotic transferences in which patients treat clinicians as though they were assassins. Accordingly, we may be able to put ourselves more firmly in positions that suggest that we can, as clinicians, provide a new mental space where new growth or new development may take place.

Summary and Conclusion

The phenomenon of the sense of disappearing in the schizophrenic must be unpacked so that we may know what the object world of the schizophrenic demands and commands. We may know how the schizophrenic capitulates, or tries to disengage himself or herself from the mandate to die and subsequently gets coopted by the object to feign a repair of the mind or restoration of the integrity of the self. For the psychoanalytic practitioner then, work in the transference must involve the therapist observing the schizophrenic's hasty assumption of the mandate to die, his or her summons to repeat in action versions of his or her mandate to disappear, and the clinician's vigilant project of putting death in its rightful place by frustrating transference demands to complicitly preserve the death sentence or captivity pronounced by the object. In this understanding of schizophrenia, a phenomenological reading of the sense of disappearing helps us to know death better so that clinicians can put it in its rightful place, that is, with the schizophrenic's anterior objects.

I shall conclude with a comparison between anorexics, trans-sexuals, and schizophrenics. I have shown elsewhere (Apprey and Stein, 1993) that the anorexic receives the injunction to die but protests that injunction simultaneously with the result that she may live, and if she does, she constantly lives at the brink of death. I have shown elsewhere (Apprey and Stein, 1993) that the transsexual psychically dies in one form but by stealth survives in another form. In schizophrenia what presents itself is a wish in the schizophrenic to submit to an injunction to die and a simultaneous complicity in feigning a restoration, a repair of the damage done to one's life. In the phenomenal world of our subjects, these three conditions are horizonal but not interchangeable. They are horizonal in terms of their experience of the urgent errand to submit to an errand toward death, but very different in terms of how they voluntarily choose to live their precarious existence.

References

Apprey, M., & Stein, H. F. (1993), *Intersubjectivity, Projective Identification, and Otherness*. Pittsburgh, PA: Duquesne University Press.

Bachelard, G. (1969), *The Philosophy of No*. New York: Orion Press.

Bowen, M. (1960), A family concept of schizophrenia. In: *The Etiology of Schizophrenia*, ed. D. D. Jackson. New York: Basic Books.

Giorgi, A. (1979), *The Relation among Level, Type, and Structure and Their Importance in Social Science Theorizing: A Dialogue with Shutz*. Duquesne Studies in Phenomenological Psychology, Vol. 3, ed. Amedeo Giorgi, R. Knowles, & L. Smith. Pittsburgh, PA: Duquesne University Press, pp. 81–96.

——— (1985), *Phenomenology and Psychological Research*. Pittsburgh, PA: Duquesne University Press.

Graumann, C. F. (1988), Phenomenological analysis and experimental method of psychology—The problem of their compatibility. *J. Theory Soc. Behav.*, 8:33–50.

Grotstein, J. S. (1983), A proposed revision of the psychoanalytic concept of primitive mental states: Part II. The borderline syndrome—Section 1: Disorders of autistic safety and symbiotic relatedness. *Contemp. Psychoanal.*, 19:570–604.

——— (1986), Schizophrenic personality disorder: ". . . And if I should die before I wake." In: *Towards a Comprehensive Model for Schizophrenic Disorders*, ed. D. B. Feinsilver. Hillsdale, NJ: Analytic Press, pp. 29–71.

Hartmann, H. (1964), *Essays on Ego Psychology.* New York: International Universities Press.

Ingarden, R. (1975), *On the Motives which Led Husserl to Transcendental Idealism,* tr. A. Hannibalsson. The Hague: Martinus Nijhoff.

Jackson, D. D., Block, J., & Peterson, U. (1958), Psychiatrists' conceptions of the schizophrenic patient. *Arch. Neurol. & Psychiatry,* 79:448–459.

Jackson, D. D., & Weakland, J. (1959), Schizophrenic symptoms and family interaction. *Arch. Gen. Psychiatry,* 1:618–621.

Kronfeld, A. (1920), *Das Wessen der Psychiatrischen Erkenntnis.* Berlin: Springer.

Lidz, R. W., & Lidz, T. (1949), The family environment of schizophrenic patients. *Amer. J. Psychiatry,* 106:322–345.

Lidz, T. (1973), *The Origin and Treatment of Schizophrenic Disorders.* New York: Basic Books.

———— Fleck, S., & Cornelison, A. (1965), *Schizophrenia and the Family.* New York: International Universities Press.

Merleau-Ponty, M. (1962), *The Phenomenology of Perception.* New York: Humanities Press.

Volkan, V. D. (1995), *The Infantile Psychotic Self and Its Fates: Understanding and Treating Schizophrenics and Other Difficult Patients.* Northvale, NJ: Jason Aronson.

Wynne, L. C., Ryckoff, I. M., Day, J., & Hirsch, S. I. (1958), Pseudomutuality in the family relations of schizophrenics. *Psychiatry,* 21:205–220.

———— Singer, M., & Bartko, J. (1975), Schizophrenics and their families: Recent research on parental communication. In: *Psychiatric Research and the Widening Perspective,* ed. J. M. Tanner. New York: International Universities Press.

5

A Room within a Room: Clinical Observations of a "Mad" Core

VAMIK D. VOLKAN, M.D.
GABRIELE AST, M.D.

A metapsychological understanding of the infantile psychotic self is presented in chapter 1. This chapter examines how the existence of such a core can be observed in a clinical setting. As stated earlier, the infantile psychotic self has various fates, among them being the development of a psychotic personality organization. Dr. Gabriele Ast's patient, Lena, has a psychotic personality organization. Lena exhibits her "seed of madness" in reenactments which have three related meanings:

1. She tries, literally, to put the infantile psychotic self in "a room within a room." This symbolically reflects her attempt to encapsulate the "seed of madness," at least partially.

111

2. She engages in activities to change the external world to fit the demands of her psychotic core so that a sense of reality is maintained.

3. She hopes to libidinally saturate and rebuild her psychotic core in order to modify its nature.

Since Lena's attempts are not successful, however, she is doomed to repeat them.

Lena Seeks Treatment

Lena, a woman in her midtwenties complaining of chest pains and headaches, went to see Dr. Ast in Germany. During their first encounter, Lena's hair was long but hidden under a hat, giving her the appearance of a young leftist worker; yet at the same time, she was clean and mannerly, and might even be considered beautiful. In spite of the fact that nothing about Lena was visibly offensive, Ast felt that something within Lena was ugly and horrible. Although she made no comment, her involuntary discomfort about the patient caught her by surprise, making her curious. Ast found herself remembering a story one of her friends had told: while washing her hair in a sink, the friend observed white maggots with red eyes crawling out of the drain and was repulsed and disgusted. Ast wondered if Lena was externalizing something horrifying onto her, without at first knowing what this horrible thing might be.

Lena reported that, until recently, she had shared an apartment with Ruth, a friend her own age. During that time, when she was 24 years old, she met a man and became pregnant within two weeks. Lena felt the pregnancy was "destiny" since her mother had also conceived her at the age of 24. Once her pregnancy became known, however, Lena's relationship with Ruth deteriorated. Lena expected Ruth to take care of her and felt frustrated when she did not. When Lena legally terminated her pregnancy, her relationship with Ruth became even more strained and bizarre. One day, while they were still living in the same apartment and seeing each other on a daily basis, Ruth left a letter for Lena on a table. In it Ruth described Lena as made up of a sticky, adhesive substance like black tar "that crawls into every crack on the surface as it spreads." Hearing Ruth's description of Lena, Ast thought that it was in accord with her own first impression of the new patient. Most likely, both had sensed Lena's "psychotic seed."

In addition to writing a letter to Lena, Ruth had begun painting monsterlike figures on the wall of her room that may have represented her perception of her roommate's hidden aspect. Ruth may have sensed that Lena's pregnancy and abortion was an attempt to reincarnate and then kill the monsters from her past, which will be described later. In any case, when Lena saw her roommate's paintings, they induced eerie feelings in her. She left the apartment and rented a room at an inn with her latest boyfriend. During this period she experienced headaches, chest pains, and occasional terrifying anxiety that prompted her to seek treatment.

It was determined that there was no evidence of a somatic basis for Lena's headaches and chest pains. In fact, these symptoms disappeared significantly after treatment began. Although one may wonder about the role of constitutional and biological factors in the establishment of Lena's psychotic seed, we believe her story offers ample evidence of the primacy of psychological factors.

Lena's story slowly emerged during her treatment. We present it here basically according to the developmental age and related events. This is in order to shed light on the reenactments that dealt with the influence of her hidden psychotic seed (the black tar) and to observe in adult language the indescribable infantile psychotic self.

Lena's Early Childhood

Lena's mother delivered a healthy baby girl at the age of 24, even though Lena's father had encouraged an abortion. Lena was eventually told by her mother of her father's desire for the abortion (her death). Given the circumstances at the time of Lena's birth, we believe that her mother's reactions, feelings, and fantasies about having a baby were also ambivalent and complicated. It was into this troubled environment that Lena was born.

At the time of Lena's birth the family was very poor. Her father was in jail for embezzling money from the company where he worked, but was released during Lena's early infancy and returned to his family. A bisexual, he spent time with other men and was away from home at various times. During the first eight months of Lena's life, her mother stayed home, living on social welfare benefits. The young mother then gave baby Lena to a foster family, but took her back after six months because she felt Lena, who was left in soiled diapers for extended periods, was not receiving proper care with the foster family.

Lena's mother stayed at home under very poor financial conditions until her daughter was 3 years old. She then returned to work at whatever jobs she could find, leaving Lena with a variety of caretakers. While in treatment, Lena recalled how she always wanted to be the child of the different individuals or families who looked after her. Our best guess is that Lena had difficulty in establishing object constancy because of the early traumas and early object losses she experienced.

"Hooking" and "Unhooking" People

At about the age of 3, when her mother began working fulltime, Lena began wandering in the woods near her family's home. Beneath the trees she would build a "cave" or "nest" with sticks and sit in it for hours, daydreaming. As an adult she could not recall the content of these daydreams, but in treatment gave various versions of her cave/nest-building and her associations with them.

One variation of Lena's "cave" or "nest" was a persistent repeating fantasy throughout her life of being alone on top of a platform which could be reached by climbing up stairs on which people sat. These people occasionally got to the top and had "contact" with Lena, but these contacts were not long-lived, and the visitors would soon descend the stairs, leaving Lena alone on the platform. The boyfriend who made Lena pregnant was also included in this fantasy. He would frantically run back and forth on the upper platform, but without having a lasting contact with Lena.

In her fantasy, Lena would throw "hooks" on the steps below "to catch people" as a fisherman catches fish. Since she claimed she could read the minds of these people, one assumes that they did not represent fully differentiated objects or their representations, but objects and representations often fused with Lena's images of herself. Later in life, she carried a notebook around with her and wrote down her conversations with others, in a sense "hooking" them with herself. Without concrete evidence (her notes) that the conversation had taken place, her relationship would disappear. Sitting in a "nest" or on the platform most probably reflected her repeated efforts to find a stable mother substitute. "Hooking" people and having temporary contacts reflected her unsatisfactory childhood relationships with various caregivers.

From a metapsychological point of view, we can state that Lena attempted to create a core self fused with the image of a substitute mother, hoping to saturate it with "good" affects. This in turn would allow her to develop object constancy. Since, however, she never succeeded in "hooking" others in a steady and continuous fashion, one supposes that her core was filled with "bad" affects instead, and her efforts to change it were frustrated over and over again.

The manifest content of such fantasies reflects the disturbances in the "channel" described in chapter 1; mother–child experiences had been inadequate. Lena tried to have "multiple mothers," but developed no lasting nurturing link with any. She was doomed to search for a nurturing object and fail, always returning to a lonely existence in the "cave" where she was both the baby and the mother. We were able to conclude that these fantasies were most likely "transitional fantasies" as described by Volkan (1976), and they reflected her object hunger, her difficulty in establishing stable object constancy, her frustrations in object relations, as well as her attempts to enlarge and stabilize her relationship with the external world. A transitional object is like a lantern with one transparent and one opaque side (Volkan, 1976). When the child wants to relate to the world, he or she turns the transparent side toward the world, illuminating it in order to get to know the environment. Conversely, when the child wants to wipe out the external environment, he or she turns the opaque side toward the world. Lena's fantasies were under her absolute control as a child controls his or her transitional objects.

In the following story, the saturation of the fused seed with "bad" aggressive affects is clearly demonstrated, and since it refers also to night dreams rather than conscious fantasies, it permits a more direct grasp of Lena's inner world.

A Repeating Nightmare

Lena started having repeated nightmares when she was 4 years of age. The dreams began with Lena playing with a teddy bear that, at the lowest level of her development, most likely represented a transitional object (Winnicott, 1953), and an experience between "not-me and mother-me" (Greenacre, 1970). The teddy bear would walk into a bathroom and climb up onto the commode and sit on the top of the water tank. (One gets a reflection of Lena's sitting on a platform in her conscious fantasies.) Then the teddy bear would become "bad" and very frightening. It is clear here that Lena's core "good" image had a tendency to turn sour and terrorizing.

Lena had no memory of her toilet training, but her mother's apparent preoccupation with the foster family's perceived failure to keep Lena in clean diapers when she was between 8 and 14 months old suggests that she may have undertaken Lena's toilet training early. The teddy bear might have been invested with anal sadism of both parent and child. Lena had been told by her mother about her father's infanticidal thoughts, and it would not be surprising if the mother also entertained them; we cannot know if she had fantasized flushing her baby down the toilet. Lena's imaginary "hooks" to catch people might be condensed with a wish to hold onto her body parts (i.e., feces).

Thoughts about bodily disintegration and death troubled little Lena. When she was 8 years old, she often took aspirin on her own to combat "headaches," using the pills as a magical inanimate antidote for her anxiety. This was a version of using a transitional object for dealing with the psychotic anxiety which Sperling (1963) described as a *childhood fetish*, and Mahler (1968) termed a *psychotic fetish*. The "headaches" and "chest pains" that brought Lena to Dr. Ast were late versions of somatic expressions of her terrorizing anxiety.

When she came to treatment, Lena had been afraid of dying suddenly and that her body would not be found, especially if she were to die in her room. Sometimes when she entered her bedroom, she felt that she entered a coffin. At such times the external world would lose its importance, while Lena, in her "coffin," would have no formal thoughts. Her thinking would be "cloudy." Her concerns seem to have had a great deal to do with her fear of losing the integrity of her body self. Sometimes she was almost too frightened to move, suggesting the possibility that she had, perhaps, experienced catatoniclike states. During Lena's treatment, Dr. Ast also considered the possibility that by being "dead" Lena felt she would please and "repair" her parents who did not wish her to be born.

Naming the Psychotic Seed

Although Lena did not have a special name for her own psychotic core, there are many examples of how patients describe their infantile psychotic selves in different ways (Volkan, 1995).

Some refer to their psychotic seeds according to the affect with which it is situated. A patient may call it "the monster in the middle of me," while others give it animal names; for example, one patient who was born on Groundhog Day sometimes perceived his infantile psychotic self as a groundhog.

Another patient, who was treated by Dr. Eli Zaler and whose case was supervised by Volkan, had six reconstructive surgical operations. This was an attempt to make her body resemble that of a cat, the animal she associated with her infantile psychotic self, in order to find a fit between her "seed of madness" and external reality. As long as there were surgeons willing to change her legs, her abdomen, and her face, she kept a sense of reality and never went into full-blown schizophrenia.

The choice of a cat as a symbol of this patient's "mad seed" was related to her childhood memory of seeing her mother smash the head of a kitten; the aggression and unnamable "bad" affects had been expressed in the horrible scene of beating the kitten. She had sensed her mother's wish that her child had never been born. By turning herself into a cat, she would be smashed and disappear, thus fulfilling her mother's unconscious wish. At the same time, her daily life centered around caring for dozens of sick cats as a way to provide a libidinal environment for the animals (her own core). Unfortunately, all the cats had feline leukemia and were doomed to die, making the patient feel that no matter what she did, she could not alter the animal's (her psychotic core's) fate.

Lena also seemed to have a sense of her infantile psychotic self as nonhuman, even though she had no specific pet name for it. She could find a fit between her psychotic core and external reality by *becoming* a bird, a bat, a dog, or a corpse in a coffin. When she was a child, she would ask older women if she could take their dogs with her while she rambled in the woods. With them she related to nonhuman objects and in caring for and identifying with them she would, by extension, "hook" herself to their owners, the older women, at best temporarily.

At home, Lena pretended to be a bat, hanging upside down for hours from an exercise bar her father had fastened in a door frame. Her mother seemed not to understand that her child's bizarre behavior was an expression of the problem Lena had in relating to other people. Once she even became angry and threw her daughter down from the bar. Lena fell on her head during this incident and had to stay in bed for days because of the pain; for her crying, Lena was then beaten by her mother.

An Effort to Become Transsexual

Dr. Ast had been struck on first acquaintance with Lena's boyish appearance, and it was later learned that Lena had, in reality, tried to be transsexual at one time. When Lena was 8 she found pornographic magazines belonging to her father with illustrations of penises, vaginas, and various heterosexual and homosexual acts. The impact of these pictures, combined with sexual advances from her father's boyfriends, brought about psychosexual trauma which, in turn, exacerbated Lena's object relations conflicts. She began wishing to be a boy and thinking that in fact she was a male trapped inside a female body. From the age of 9 to 14 years, Lena dressed like a boy, carried a knife, and acted like a young transsexual.

Through their work with *true* transsexuals, Volkan and his coworkers (Volkan, 1980, 1995; Volkan and Greer, 1995) showed that such individuals have infantile psychotic selves. Through surgery, usually through multiple operations, they try to create an illusion of a genital, and then a total body fusion between their self representation and the representation of a "good" mother. The true transsexual does not simply want to become a person of the opposite sex but wants to be an idealized version of a me-"good"-mother unit.

Because of Lena's gender confusion, let us briefly describe an example of a "true" female transsexual:

The early mother of a true female transsexual has been depressed. Her daughter develops an unconscious fantasy of becoming her mother's penis and repairing her body in order to lessen her mother's depression so she can, in turn, nurture her child. Through surgery she hopes to accomplish at least a "good" genital body fusion which will in turn enable her self to start all over with a libidinally saturated core self representation. Unfortunately, surgery does not provide lasting intrapsychic structural change. Volkan and Masri (1989) describe a young true female transsexual who developed a fantasy of having a penis in response to her mother's sexual hunger. Lena's mother was similarly deprived of her husband's penis due to his bisexuality and absences from home. Among "true" female transsexuals we often notice a fantasy of responding to their mother's perceived sexual hunger by having a penis.

Going through the adolescent passage (Blos, 1979) ended Lena's transsexual tendencies, but her present way of dressing indicated remnants of her desire to become a boy. This, along with her thinking and behaving as though she were one, remained with her until she sought treatment. However, the adolescent passage and Lena's corresponding struggle of "second individuation" (Blos, 1979), reignited her search for a new "good" mother and "good" experiences to start a new seed. She found a woman named Erika, who was in her fifties, and transferred the psychodynamics of her unconscious fantasy of being a female transsexual to the psychodynamics of her experiences with Erika.

A Room within a Room

For about four years Lena idealized Erika, intrapsychically leading a symbioticlike life with her, although physically she remained in her parental home, carrying out her daily functions with her healthier self, without succumbing to a crystallized psychosis. Lena visited Erika every day and did the cooking and cleaning for her, making it difficult to distinguish who was the mother figure and who was the child. In Lena's mind the two representations were fused. (At the age of 10 she had experienced a similar but briefer experience with another older woman whose child she had wanted to be.)

Lena and Erika created a special room, a reflection of Lena's "cave," "nest," or platform, that symbolized her externalized infantile psychotic self and her attempts to modify it. The creation of this special room was not a first for Lena but was a new version of her childhood's "room within a room." Little Lena had often built a "room within a room" by partitioning off a section of her bedroom. She did not recall exactly when she started to do this, but she was sure she had always done so. She would enter her "room within a room" and stay there for hours. She was then unaware of the "other" (real) world. Her "room within a room" seems to have been an external reflection of her partially encapsulated psychotic seed.

At 17, Lena asked Erika if she might move into her house. When Erika replied by saying, "I don't want to mother another child," to Lena it meant no hope for having a "good" mother and a "good" core. Lena was devastated. She retreated to her bed and "disappeared" for many weeks.

"Disappearing"

The act of disappearing when rejected by Erika reminded Lena of her earlier responses to another frustration in the third grade. She had been having trouble with mathematics and felt rejected by her teacher, so she "disappeared" and hid in the basement of her parent's house and did not go to school until it was discovered that she was missing.

Lena's "disappearing" had also occurred on other occasions. Once while in kindergarten, she had been punished by a caretaker who suspected her of eating Christmas pudding without permission. Angered by this unjust punishment, Lena "disappeared" under a table. Those in charge of the kindergarten looked for her everywhere, and finally called the police. She was not found until she emerged from her hiding place on her own. Lena recalled that while in hiding she had experienced bodily sensations, including feeling big; she was inflating her body self as well as her omnipotence. The hiding seems to have represented another "room within a room" experience.

Lena also had many conscious wishes about disappearing; for example, when frustrated by her boyfriend she fantasized about jumping into a river, disappearing, and coming out a "new Lena." Thus, some of Lena's acts of "disappearing" were usually accompanied by "new birth" fantasies. We believe that her death–rebirth wishes may have been a response to her father's (parent's) wish that she had died and vanished from her mother's womb (see Apprey, chapter 4). By becoming *nothing* (disappearing), she could please her parents, and in a sense "repair" them; then she could be reborn to parents who wanted her and who did not want her dead. Lena had reenacted a version of this unconscious fantasy by becoming pregnant at 24 and destroying her fetus. She had killed the fetus/herself-as-a-fetus (a "monster") to repair her parents in the hope of being "reborn" and evolving a libidinally saturated infantile self.

Through her relationship with Erika, Lena most likely hoped for further development of her core self. The sudden termination of this attempt caused her to find new reenactments.

Greece

Rejected by Erika, Lena stayed in her room for weeks, eating chocolates that she associated with feces. Her absence from school resulted in her expulsion. If this represented a sort of "death," she eventually came to life again and bought new clothes, new books, and other personal items. But her "newness" was short lived, and when she became angry at someone or something, such as her boyfriend's image, she wanted to hang herself or cut off her own fingers.

Lena eventually went to Greece, which, in her mind, was "blue, yellow, round, and warm." Greece was the new "good" mother-breast while Germany (her mother, Erika, chocolates), which she left behind, remained "brown, square, and cold." She found a young lover in Greece who composed love songs for her and she made some money by drawing and selling landscapes. During sex with the young Greek, as well as with others at different times, Lena would have unusual sensations, experiencing sexual union as something like "Dracula eating my internal soul." "Badness" saturated the representation and she felt that sex was disgusting. At other times, she would merge with her partner and "disappear," feeling his orgasm as her own. At such times she would actually reach orgasm herself.

After staying in Greece for a few months, she then returned to Germany. The young Greek's response to this was to cut himself, not fatally, and to threaten to cut Lena's throat to protest their separation. As with other relationships, this intimacy and separation experience also included "bad" affects and murderous impulses.

Living in a Castle

On her return to Germany, Lena moved in with an 80-year-old man who lived in a castle that, walled off from the rest of the world, became another version of a "nest." The old man, in turn, was the long-sought "good" mother figure. During this same time, Lena's mother attempted suicide. It seemed that the unconscious idea of "murder" persisted in their relationship, and when Lena found a "new" mother (the old man), her symbiotic (biological) mother had to die. Lena's mother was admitted to a psychiatric hospital where she remained for a year.

Lena walked around the castle unclothed and felt like a princess. The (naked) baby–mother unit, saturated with "good" libidinal feelings was established. It was an external reenactment of a "good" seed of self that would enable her to start life all over again. When a guest came to visit the old man in the castle, he spoiled Lena's efforts; the castle was no longer "a room within a room" that she could control and saturate with "good" feelings.

Disappointed and full of "bad" feelings, Lena tried at once to create another externalized version of the infantile self. She "created" a place for herself in the castle by moving a heavy wooden wardrobe across a hallway to mark off and link her living area from the rest of the castle. By closing the front door of the wardrobe behind her, she would leave the wardrobe through an opening in its back, and enter her "room within a room," which was now hidden from other people.

The cruelty of the real world, however, continued to intrude into Lena's life. The old man, who had once been Erika's lover, married Erika's older daughter, a lesbian twenty years Lena's senior. Yet Lena knew this woman's secret—although married, she maintained a lesbian relationship. But in order to keep the old man happy and "good," Lena lied about this knowledge and "protected" him. Soon, however, everything became complicated and Erika's daughter, as her mother had done earlier, rejected Lena, banishing her from the castle, and leaving her and her core once more flooded with rage.

Treatment

After she left the castle, Lena tried to idealize and reenact symbiotic relationships with three other older women, but failed. Between these disappointments she would go to Greece to experience that country as a "good" mother, at least temporarily. Her biological mother made more attempts at suicide; Lena moved in with Ruth, became pregnant, destroyed the fetus, separated from Ruth, and then came to see Dr. Ast.

Although fascinated by Lena, Dr. Ast knew that she was unlikely to respond to psychoanalytic psychotherapy in a "typical" way. Yet she thought that without such treatment Lena might not have a chance for a "normal" or at least a less turbulent life, so she arranged to work with her. Lena then "disappeared" after the fifth session (without saying she was going to Greece). Dr. Ast was out of touch with her for three months and knew nothing of her whereabouts or condition. When Lena reappeared, she established a self-imposed "time limit" on her treatment by agreeing to work with Dr. Ast for one year, twice a week, until she finished her baccalaureate; after that she would go to Greece for good, if she wished. Lena, afraid that her new relationship would turn sour like her other intimate experiences, wanted to control the situation and get out of it before it became "bad." Dr. Ast explained to Lena that the therapist did not have a "time limit" and that Lena could talk about her impulse to "disappear" in treatment rather than actually "disappearing" physically. They began to work together again and the analyst slowly became more familiar with Lena's inner world.

Analysis revealed that Lena was not schizophrenic; she was able to test reality, especially when no intimacy was required. She had a functioning ego that allowed her to behave appropriately while working as a model, mostly posing nude for artists, and to resume her schoolwork. Ast noted Lena's healthier part, with its associated ego mechanisms, repeatedly "created" experiences the patient perceived as intimate in order to respond to the three demands of the infantile psychotic self:

1. Partially to encapsulate and attempt to split off the infantile psychotic self from the rest of the personality organization in order for Lena to function as an adult in everyday life.

2. At the same time, absorb the psychotic core and become involved in many "reenactments" that would provide a fit between the demands of the infantile psychotic self and the external world, yielding a sense of reality.

3. Be involved in repeated activities that would attempt to replace the infantile psychotic self with a new (fused) self, saturated with "good" affects. Lena repeatedly failed to accomplish this and the infantile psychotic self—saturated with "bad" affects—persisted.

In treatment, Ast's office quickly became another version of a "room within a room," a symbolic externalized location of the infantile psychotic self where "not-me" and "mother-me" (Greenacre, 1970) met. Trying to pump "good" affects into this setting, Lena saw Ast's office as filled with clouds, but she could feel the analyst's presence. She often experienced variations of the Isakower phenomenon (Isakower, 1938) and had described shadowy balloonlike images while in a hypnagogic state. The images came nearer and nearer, as though they would fill her mouth. Isakower connected this feeling with memory traces of breast-feeding and early ego organization. In Lena's experience, Ast's office would slowly fill with a "swollen something" (a breast) that came closer and closer to her mouth (see Lehtonen, chapter 2).

Lena rented a cello while in treatment and learned how to play it. Ast sensed that the cello represented herself, the analyst; Lena kept her analyst with her by holding it. She could thus deny separation, and maintain a kind of object constancy by utilizing a prop. Lena described how she would put her arms around the cello and feel its body fused with her own. She was trying to create "good" music. As treatment continued, Lena also began to "hook" Ast in other ways, and to concretize her "link" with the analyst; Lena wanted to record their conversations in a notebook. As noted earlier, she had used much the same method as a child, trying to maintain contact and to achieve object constancy with the external world. Lena also wanted to bring a tape recorder to her sessions. Instead, the analyst encouraged Lena to verbalize her impulses to Ast so that they could communicate more directly.

When one year passed (the time limit Lena had established), she was still in treatment. However, as Lena's treatment progressed into its second year, Ast had to leave her office for a month for professional reasons. Upon learning of the anticipated separation, Lena began to speak of returning to Greece again and disappearing. Ast interpreted this to mean that Lena planned to replace her with Greece, and she suggested that they continue to talk about Lena's impulse to disappear, allowing the "bad" affect to surface in their sessions. Ast added that she could tolerate Lena's negative feelings about her, and explained that her month-long absence was not due to a malignant design on the analyst's part. Ast further explained that Lena was not pushing the analyst away, she simply had a previously planned professional commitment. She then suggested they try to look at the situation together to see that it was not "murdering" either them or their relationship.

Both analyst and patient came to understand Lena's genuine attempt to achieve object constancy for her core, and Lena began to show signs of separation anxiety in more normal and adaptive ways. This was a good progressive sign. When Ast returned to work after a month's absence, Lena kept her first two appointments, but then left for Greece. During their last session together, Dr. Ast was able to tell Lena that she had become, in her patient's eyes, another rejecting caretaker. She repeated that her absence was not a malignant design and that it was not Lena who caused Dr. Ast's absence from the office. While the patient was able to "hear" the analyst's explanations, she felt that she could not tolerate staying with Dr. Ast. Lena was filled with "bad" affects and felt such affects could destroy both the patient and the analyst. Lena said she did not wish to terminate her treatment but felt she had to get away for a while in order to have any hope of working with Dr. Ast in the future. Dr. Ast understood Lena's dilemma. They agreed to make the following arrangement: The analyst would keep one appointment for Lena at a specific time each month. Lena, in turn, would call from Greece and inform Dr. Ast whether or not she would keep that appointment. This arrangement was an unusual therapeutic parameter. But Lena's case was unusual and Dr. Ast wanted to be able to save the relationship.

For five months Lena informed Dr. Ast she would not keep her appointment. But, in the sixth month she returned to her treatment and once more the therapist and the patient "resumed" their routine work. Dr. Ast learned that before going to Greece, Lena, in spite of her poor finances, had bought the cello (the analyst's "good" representation) which she had previously been renting. While in Greece, Lena had the "good" analyst with her. The physical distance between Germany and Greece represented a psychological distance between the "good" and "bad" relationships, and the "good" relationship could thus be maintained and not destroyed by the "bad" one.

Dr. Ast also learned that Lena had done a great deal of internal work during her time in Greece, assimilating many insights which she had learned in treatment. Lena informed Dr. Ast she now had a specific name for her core. Previously, this had been identified as a "black tar," a "monster," or an animal, and Lena had acted it out in various ways, such as by pretending to be a bat. Now she called it "the hurt child" within her bosom—an appropriate reference to her being hurt by Dr. Ast's one-month absence. The name "the hurt child" also stood for her infantile self which, in reality, was injured, and reflected an improvement in Lena's condition. The core was no longer a "monster" or an animal; it was humanized now. Lena's treatment was then able to move to a new plateau.

The Name of the Rose

During a session early in Lena's treatment, Ast found herself spontaneously recalling the film *The Name of the Rose*. The film, which Ast had seen before Lena began treatment, involved murder and intrigue in Medieval Europe. Although Ast could not recall many exact details of the film, or fully analyze the images that connected it to her patient, she felt that beneath Lena's roselike appearance lurked something archaic and murderous, hidden, and sinister.

When we decided to write about Lena's case, our curiosity about *The Name of the Rose* increased, and we arranged to watch it. Eventually we also read the book by Umberto Eco on which the movie is based and from which the movie derives its title. We were surprised to note that a central part of the film's plot concerned "a room within a room." We were able to detect various possible interpretations of different symbols, plots, and subplots, with some interesting relevance to Lena's internal world.

In the film, a learned Franciscan, Brother William of Baskerville, played by Sean Connery, investigates mysterious deaths in a medieval abbey. The center of the investigation focuses on a secret library—a room within a room. The library, a labyrinth, is laid out on a plan which none of the monks in the abbey are called upon to know. Only the librarian has received the secret from the librarian who preceded him. In turn he would communicate the secret, while still alive, to his assistant.

Some monks who seem to be preoccupied with the secrets of the library are murdered. Brother William and his assistant, a young Benedictine novice, find the secret entrance to the library, enter it and discover the existence of Aristotle's second book of the *Poetics*. The book was kept hidden because it contains an antidote for fear: laughter (good affects), and because its secrets could threaten man's fear of God. Eco (1980) describes a dialogue between Brother William and a monk named Jorge who in the long run turns out to be the villain. William says, "I believe laughter is a good medicine to treat humors and other afflictions of the body, melancholy in particular" (p. 149). Jorge responds that, "Laughter shakes the body, distorts the features of the face, makes man similar to the monkey" (p. 149).

The copy of Aristotle's *Poetics* is further safeguarded with poison so that anyone who turns the pages will be contaminated and die. We imagined that the secret library described an infantile core where the libidinal (laughter) core was saturated with aggression (poison).

In the midst of the film's intrigue and murder, a young peasant girl takes off her filthy clothes, revealing her beautiful body. She and the young novice have intercourse, and though he is infatuated, he follows his religious calling and never has intercourse again. The film ends when he speaks as an old man about his only sexual encounter and his love for the peasant girl. Eco wrote of the novice's description of her image, "my soul had not forgotten her face, and could not manage to feel that this memory was perverse: rather, it throbbed as if in that face shone all the bliss of creation" (p. 332). Throughout the years, he had turned to her image again and again for solace and perhaps in longing for lost pleasure, reminding us of Lena's repeated attempts to find a good mother without ever succeeding.

Of course, it is not possible to say if Ast unconsciously perceived Lena's psychological room within a room soon after they began working together. She may have simply recalled the filth, poverty, murders, and other offensive events depicted in the film when she sensed Lena's internal world beneath her clean appearance. These aspects of why *The Name of the Rose* came to Ast's mind in the early phase of Lena's treatment, and Ast's unconsciously noting the symbol between the story of the film and the case of Lena, may always remain a mystery. However, we do know that, at the present time, analyst and patient are aware of what is in Lena's secret room. Such knowledge is the first but crucial step toward the patient's attempt at psychological structural change.

References

Blos, P. (1979), *The Adolescent Passage*. New York: International Universities Press.

Eco, U. (1980), *The Name of the Rose,* tr. W. Weaver. New York: Warner Books.

Greenacre, P. (1970), The transitional object and the fetish: with special reference to the role of illusion. *Internat. J. Psycho-Anal.*, 51:447–456.

Isakower, O. (1938), A contribution to the patho-psychology of phenomena associated with falling asleep. *Internat. J. Psycho-Anal.*, 10:331–345.

Mahler, M. S. (1968), *On Human Symbiosis and the Vicissitudes of Individuation.* New York: International Universities Press.

Sperling, M. (1963), Fetishism in children. *Psychoanal. Quart.*, 32:374–392.

Volkan, V. D. (1976), *Primitive Internalized Object Relations: A Clinical Study of Schizophrenic, Borderline, and Narcissistic Patients.* New York: International Universities Press.

——— (1980), Transsexualism as examined from the viewpoint of internalized object relations. In: *On Sexuality: Psychoanalytic Observations,* ed. T. B. Karasu & C. W. Socarides. New York: International Universities Press, pp. 199–221.

——— (1995), *The Infantile Psychotic Self and Its Fates: Understanding and Treating Schizophrenics and Other Difficult Patients.* Northvale, NJ: Jason Aronson.

——— & Greer, W. F. (1995), True transsexualism. In: *Sexual Deviations,* 3rd ed., ed. I. Rosen. London: Oxford University Press, pp. 158–173.

——— & Masri, A. (1989), The development of female transsexualism. *Amer. J. Psychother.*, 43:92–107.

Winnicott, D. (1953), Transitional objects and transitional phenomena. *Internat. J. Psycho-Anal.*, 34:89–97.

6

A Crocodile in a Pouch

Gabriele Ast, M.D.

The aim of this chapter is to provide clinical illustrations of
the theoretical concepts discussed in the preceding four chapters: the infantile psychotic self, early body image, and inter-
generational transmission. I describe the case of Karl, in whom
obsessive–compulsive symptoms enveloped his "seed of madness" (Volkan, 1995) and the sum of his bodily symptoms became a "spokesperson" of it. Karl sensed the existence of his
infantile psychotic self as an undifferentiated and dangerous
being in a container, a crocodile in a pouch. Karl's case allows
us to see clearly the internalizations of one's interaction with
one's early environment, and the contamination of such internalizations with unconscious fantasies.

Karl's Symptoms

Karl is a bachelor who lives in Munich, Germany, where I practice. Suffering from painful cramps in his abdomen, which

he had first experienced as a 3½-year-old child, he entered analysis with me at the age of 40. According to Karl, during his first childhood bout, the symptoms had disappeared a few months after they had begun, but they resumed again when he was 17. Since then they had occurred on a daily basis. The intensification of his symptoms and the fear that he would always remain single and lonely brought him to treatment. As he began treatment, he was working as a legal counselor for clients interested in early retirement.

Karl's bodily symptoms were accompanied by obsessive–compulsive actions. In the morning, upon leaving the house for work, he would be plagued by the idea that he had forgotten something, and his fear would lead to painful cramps. He would return home, where he would not know what he was looking for, and this would make his cramps persist. To ease the cramps he would walk the long distance to work, avoiding the subway (the significance of Karl's avoidance of the subway will be discussed later in this chapter). When reading a book for his work, if the need arose to consult another for comparison, his cramps would start. When drinking tea, the thought of finishing the cup would again provoke cramps. Yet a decision to leave some tea in the cup would also lead to bodily troubles. When shopping for personal things, Karl would purchase two of the same item, such as two identical pairs of shoes or trousers. One pair he would leave in the closet for future use, but the thought of actually using this second pair would induce anxiety and symptoms. He never wore the extra shoes or trousers.

In general, what triggered Karl's daily symptoms was any decision or action to leave a location or possession, or to complete a task. He lived life as though there were "two worlds," behaving as though caught between a half full and an empty teacup, between the pair of shoes he was wearing and the pair in the closet he could wear but would not. His obsessionalism was generalized, and in some situations his preoccupation with what to leave behind and what to embark upon was not readily discernible. However, closer scrutiny indicated that changing locations, things, and tasks always generated remarkable stress for Karl. Leaving a comb "by mistake" on his bed, for example, would start his cramps because the comb was in a "wrong" location. But opening the door of the bathroom, which adjoined his bedroom, to put the comb in its "correct" place would also induce cramps because the open door would spoil his orderly bedroom. Furthermore, he did not want the smell of the bathroom to intrude into the bedroom. It was as if the border between the two locations might collapse.

Karl was also very interested in a "philosophical" question which, according to him, had preoccupied the ancient Greeks: whether time moved from one discrete point to another or flowed continuously without stopping at various points. If the first idea was correct, an arrow aimed at a running man would never hit him because the man would have left the point prior to the arrival of the arrow at the same location. However, if time moved along a continuum, the arrow, moving faster than the man, would hit him.

Beneath his existence in "two worlds" Karl sensed a "black thing" in him which, he thought, could suck in or eat people. This "black thing" usually had no form, but sometimes he perceived it as a small black coffin that changed in size. Sometimes the coffin had a small white ball in it, and sometimes, a baby. When the "black thing" sucked in or ate people, Karl would sense an identification with the person eaten. For example, one of his clients, who developed cancer, reminded him of a beloved uncle from his childhood who had died from cancer. While interacting with this client, Karl would sense his "black thing" eating the man, "greedily sucking in the illness," and then Karl began to develop the man's symptoms. Eventually, what went into the "black thing" would dissolve. Karl compared the dissolution to a spider eating a bug and the bug disappearing as it became part of the spider. Thus, after being eaten by Karl, eventually the client and his cancer would dissolve in Karl's core.

Karl described his internal world in the following way. He said that he has an "internal nucleus" surrounded by an "external cover." The "internal nucleus" is his *true* being; it should not have contact with people and things because they might alter his true being. He considered his "external cover" stable, and he felt that he used this layer of himself to talk to other people. Functioning in this layer, however, necessitated learning everything *twice*, as if to prepare for living in "two worlds" at once.

In spite of his peculiar internal experiences, Karl did not have a generalized psychosis, such as schizophrenia. In his daily life he maintained contact with reality, and people in casual contact with him did not know about or notice Karl's symptoms or internal personal problems.

Karl's History Through a Psychoanalytic Lens

The following history of my patient comes from my three years of analytic work with him. As I describe his life events I will also comment on their meanings as I formulated them during our work.

Karl's father and mother were Germans born in Hungary between the World Wars (around the mid-1920s and mid-1930s respectively). Some two hundred years prior to their births, both parents' ancestors had come to Hungary to escape religious oppression. They belonged to a close-knit group of Germans living in Hungary with their own rigid traditions. Although both of Karl's parents were children of farmers in the same district, they did not know each other while in Hungary.

When Karl's father was an adolescent, Karl's paternal grandfather developed Nazi sentiments, even though such sentiments were frowned upon by the neighbors, most of whom were German. After Nazi Germany conquered Hungary, it conscripted Karl's father and grandfather into the SS. Both of them, however, soon were captured by the Russians, and interred in a prisoner of war camp in the Soviet Union for three years. There they suffered humiliation and terror, but eventually both men returned to Hungary.

The political situation in Hungary changed after the war and Germans were no longer welcome in Communist-run Hungary; most were exiled. Furthermore, Karl's family farm no longer existed. Consequently, even though he could stay in Hungary legally, Karl's father's life there was over. So he fled from Hungary to East Germany where he joined a group of former Germans from his district in Hungary who had settled in an "island" within East Germany. There Karl's father met his future wife, whose family also had fled from Hungary. At that time she was in love with a young man, an "outsider" whose family lived in the vicinity but who were not members of the settlement of Germans from Hungary. Her mother did not want her daughter to marry an "outsider." If her daughter did so, they would lose their social status and emotional attachment to the group. She considered it so crucial that her daughter marry an "insider" that she arranged for Karl's mother, then 20, to marry Karl's father, aged 32, even though they did not know each other well. After eighteen months, Karl was born to an unhappy and, most likely, depressed mother.

Around the time of Karl's birth, Karl's father began to contemplate another move, this time to escape to West Germany. Some of the members of the German group from Hungary had already escaped to West Germany, where they had formed a new settlement. Karl's mother did not want to leave her mother, but her husband persisted with his desire to escape, and she went along with the planning of it. The plans had to be kept secret; the German authorities would have punished Karl's parents if they had discovered their plan to escape.

One of the most interesting aspects of Karl's early childhood was his toilet training, which his mother later told him was accomplished by the age of 6 weeks. As an adult, Karl suspected that this was, biologically speaking, impossible.

However, his mother persisted in saying that it had, indeed, been completed at 6 weeks. She explained that she had constantly watched him for signs of certain bodily movements, whereupon she took off his diapers, gripped him under his arms, held him over a toilet, and waited until he urinated or defecated. Hearing this, Karl realized that early in his life his unhappily married and probably depressed mother had used him to express or resolve her own psychological problems. "Apparently my body did not have any privacy," he said. From infancy on, Karl had the perception that he served as his parent's "garbage can," (his phrase) meaning as a reservoir of their "bad" feelings. When held above a toilet, he was to dump out his mother's, or both of his parents' anxiety (urine and feces). Then the parents would flush away their child's (and their own) waste material down the toilet drain! His mother "taught" little Karl how to use his own abdominal muscles to rid his mother of bad feelings, namely, anxiety and depression.

Karl had a traumatic relationship with the representation of his symbiotic mother and her mothering methods. He, of course, had no conscious memory of it. However, when he described the variations of his core self representation, the "black thing," traces of his early interaction with his mother revealed themselves. "There is a 'being' in me which was created when I was created. It has no form," he would say. Then he would relate his fantasy of putting his finger in the anus of this "being" and manipulating the anus. (Karl does not recall if his mother used enemas or other manipulations.) "First, I sense the 'being' in me, then I am in the 'being'; we become interchangeable." Karl's mother had intruded into the autonomy of his body functions and added meaning to his abdominal sensations far beyond the normal indicators of the physiological readiness to urinate or defecate. The "black thing," or the "being" represented Karl's core self representation flooded with "bad" feelings. At a higher level, I believe, it also stood symbolically for a piece of feces.

His early caretakers, his mother, and her mother who lived nearby, went one step further, however. They also interfered with the child's psychological desires and needs. In an atmosphere where his adult caretakers felt frustrated by the impossibility of negotiating or bargaining their planned departure with the East German authorities, they in turn gave the little boy no room to negotiate and bargain his own wishes and needs. If Karl said "Ich will" ("I want"), his grandmother, who knew of her daughter and son-in-law's "secret plans," would say "will (want) is dead." The connection between the German verb and the name pronounced in the same way made will or Will seem like a person. At least Karl perceived Will (the proper German name is Willie) as a person; it represented him whenever he had a psychological wish or need. During his treatment, Karl one day declared that Will had somehow survived, but he (it) was crippled for life. He compared his infantile self to a tree growing on a high mountain where the air is thin (lacking psychological nutrition) and where a tree could only survive as a dwarfed one (deformed infantile self-representation).

Karl reported a dream that, I believe, symbolically illustrates his infantile psychotic self, and the role of his mother in relation to it. In the dream his mother has her arms stretched out before her, holding in her hands a baby (Karl). The baby is made of fragile glass. The vulnerability and the coldness of the glass baby whose mother performs her mothering function "at arm's length" seemed to epitomize his history with her. He also reported a fantasy that demonstrates how women continued to traumatize him after the initial years of his life, when he could perceive their aggression on a phallic level too. As an adult, one day Karl lay in the grass in a park. There he had a fantasy that a female dog attacked him and ate his penis. Now possessing his penis, the dog raped him. In other fantasies he would imagine his mother as phallic, someone holding a spear. She would then cut off Karl's arms and legs and swaddle Karl's whole amputated body, with only his mouth showing. Karl would be rendered to a "mouth self" during which time he experienced gender confusion. He would be both male and female (a castrated boy in a symbiotic relationship with his mother).

When Karl was about 3, his mother became pregnant with her second child. This pregnancy and the birth of Karl's brother frustrated his father immensely. He even accused his wife of becoming pregnant by another man. The pregnancy complicated their plans to escape from East Germany. A few weeks before the birth of Karl's one and only sibling, Karl, now 3½ years old, experienced his first abdominal cramps. Perhaps he identified with his pregnant mother, or else expressed his father's hostility toward the fetus, or simply exhibited his own jealous feelings concerning the sibling in his mother's belly. In any case, it should be recalled that his mother had "trained" him to dump out his caretakers' "bad" feelings by using his abdominal muscles. He might, therefore, attempt to get rid of a fantasized baby/feces the same way. Whatever the reasons, the abdominal symptoms became severe enough for hospitalization. The physicians thought at first that he had appendicitis, but they later discharged him without surgery.

There were constant fights at home. Since they had a very small apartment, Karl could not be protected from the commotion in his environment. In retrospect, Karl believed that during this period his parents' desire to flee East Germany began to absorb anxieties about other issues. The politically induced danger his parents feared was real. Anyone caught trying to escape from East Germany went to jail, and their children were put up for forced adoption. As a child Karl sensed all their fear and anxiety, including his mother's hesitance about leaving her own mother, and both parents' ambivalence toward their children. But his parents never verbally shared their "secret" with Karl for fear he might talk to others about it. They left Karl to internalize the content and the affects of the "secret" himself.

When Karl was 4 years old, the family managed to flee to West Germany, traveling first on a train and then on a subway. Although Karl can recall very few details of the escape, he does recall seeing a policeman. His parents later told him that he had asked if the policeman was going to catch them. Therefore, we can surmise that he knew of his parents' secret and their associated fears, and could have expressed his rage against them by somehow communicating their plan to the policeman so that he would punish them; instead, he remained silent. As I mentioned earlier, Karl eased his abdominal cramps by walking to work instead of taking the subway; the unconscious process behind his choice might have arisen from his connection of the subway to the anxieties of the family's escape from East Germany.

Upon arrival in West Germany, the family lived in a refugee camp where Karl one day "lost" his parents and experienced extreme helplessness. Shortly thereafter Karl began to exhibit some of the classic signs of the obsessive–compulsive personality as described in the well-known paper by Abraham (1924). For instance, Karl became a "clean" and obedient child, who controlled the expression of his feelings.

Karl felt lonely in their new location, and missed the friends he had left behind. The only child with whom he still maintained contact besides his brother was a female cousin his age, whose family had also escaped from East Germany. However, she kept her distance from Karl because of his obsessiveness and preoccupation with cleanliness. For example, Karl demanded to play only "clean" games—he was not fun to have around.

As Karl went through the latency period, he carried a ruler with which he took precise measurements of certain items in his environment. Precise measurements meant knowing and controlling. Later, as a prepubescent, he began to feel sexually aroused by retaining his feces. Some evidence exists that his mother continued to stimulate his anal functions; for example, during this period his mother paid inordinate attention to the cleanliness of his underpants. As an adolescent, he suffered from painful and life-threatening pleuritis and myocarditis, which were successfully treated. Before these illnesses began, he had experienced his first erection and ejaculation, and now he linked this event to his illness; he wanted to ask his physicians how "bad" the fluid was that came out of his penis, but he did not dare. In his mind ejaculations and urine seemed interchangeable. Since he associated "bad" feelings with urine, he associated them with ejaculation too. He also associated the pains in his chest with the anxieties of his past, regarding them as punishment for his unwanted sexual impulses and the disdain he felt for his parents. The pains induced in him a renewed expectation of death.

Soon after his recovery, Karl, now in his teens, turned to religion with the hope that it would control his internal world and his "bad" feelings (such as his unexpressed rage) and "bad" activities (such as his compulsive masturbation). His internal rage never ceased to exist and he obsessively masturbated almost nightly from age 14 to 24. At the age of 15, "eye contact" with a girl sexually excited him. At the age of 18, he had sexual intercourse for the first time, even though this violated the beliefs of the religion he practiced. So he made a reversal; he no longer believed in the existence of God. With "God" gone, he began to have severe anxiety attacks. His abdominal cramps resumed. He had returned to his childhood method of ridding himself of "bad" feelings. Although he was hospitalized in the psychosomatic unit of a hospital for six months, his symptoms did not disappear.

In the following years he alternated between believing that God did not exist and being extremely religious. Once he went to Rome to inquire about theological schools so that he could eventually become the pope. After exemption from military service because of his "functional working disturbance," he went from school to school studying diplomacy, law, and theology, but never staying in any school, work, or location for more than three years, and never completing a task. Even though he never finished the requirements involved in any of these careers, he had chosen them carefully—the topics he studied held emotional meanings for him. Theology related to his wish to (re-)create "God" as an external force to control his internal world. Law and diplomacy, too, functioned to control his inner world, and they also related to his wish to reconcile mother and father, East and West, and his "two worlds." But the act of comparison and negotiation involved in these studies made him anxious because he saw it as destabilizing the borders between conflicted parties. At the end Karl found employment as a legal counselor. He advised clients on how they could retire early by collecting money for damages that had occurred during their lives. Unconsciously, Karl wanted to advise *himself* and get compensation for the damages he had received. This pseudosublimation, however, did not ease his misery.

An Initial Formulation

Karl's informative history helps to explain the source of his symptoms and his personality organization. For the sake of simplicity, let me divide his symptoms into two categories: obsessive–compulsive symptoms, and bodily symptoms. I shall address the obsessive–compulsive symptoms first.

Before Karl's birth and during his early childhood, his parents and their ancestors had left one "world" and started life in "another world" under the duress of political oppression. But an "arrow" seemed to chase them, for if caught fleeing or attempting later to revisit, severe consequences would follow. For Karl, this situation recreated itself in his idea of life in two "opposing" worlds that had to be mentally kept apart, otherwise a weakness in the "border" separating them, that is, East Germany and West Germany, would generate complications.

At the same time, we know that Karl's mother did not want to leave East Germany. She wanted to stay connected to it.

Therefore, through his symptoms, Karl not only tried to un-link East and West, but he tried, paradoxically, to link them, too. In other words, he not only wanted time to travel from one discrete point to another (for a safe escape), but he also wanted time to be continuous, so that East and West could stay connected. His preoccupation with time resulted from his ef-forts to have these mental borders both "there" and "not there."

Even though they thought they had kept the "secret" from Karl, his parents' thoughts, anxieties, and ambivalence trans-mitted to Karl anyway. The *content* of the "secret" (changing location) became a key element in Karl's obsessive–compulsive symptoms. It also became intertwined with the content of Karl's psychosexual developmental problems, which fixated at the anal phase.

Karl's bodily symptoms related to his parents' anxieties in a linked, but slightly different way. His abdominal cramps reflected parental intrusion of his body image ("garbage can") and body function. The physical elimination of bodily waste material assumed a psychological function: the elimination of anxiety or the opposite, the expression of sadism. In turn nearness to feces (toilet) induced anxiety because of the per-sonal meaning of the feces and urine for Karl.

Both types of Karl's symptoms also linked with his personal-ity organization. Boyer (1961, 1983) and Volkan (1976, 1995) have described a concept which they named "reaching up." This concept describes how some patients with disturbances in self representation and early object relations "reach up" to a more advanced step in the developmental ladder and cling to it in order not to go back. These individuals, for ex-ample, exhibit open oedipal issues when what really makes them anxious is difficulty in separation-individuation. Per-sons with infantile psychotic selves, as described in chapters 1 and 5 of this volume, sometimes "reach up" to anal fixa-tions. Obsessive–compulsive behavior may dominate their clinical pictures, but not because of a regression from the dif-ficulties of oedipal issues; instead, their behavior stems from controlling the disturbances in the self and object relations at the oral level. Karl's behavior fit this pattern. Furthermore, his mother stimulated his anal functions when he was a baby at the oral level—a tacit encouragement to "reach up." Karl's bodily symptoms, as indicated earlier, became the nonverbal discharges of his symbiotic core.

I see two types of splits in Karl's personality organization. The first one came from encapsulating his infantile psychotic self, which was symbiotically related to the representation of his mother. This self, infused with anxiety and rage, used body language to discharge tension. Karl called this self his "black thing," his "black coffin with a white ball," his "internal nucleus," or his "being." This "nucleic self" stayed separate from the other self representation that enveloped it. The "envelope self" included a second split, as evidenced by his preoccupation with "two worlds."

While Karl's history begins to explain his symptoms, the transference-related material from his treatment with me provides an even more powerful illustration of his internal world. First I will report further material illuminating his symptoms, and then I will show how his infantile psychotic self appeared in his treatment.

Karl's Attempt to Move from One Location to Another During Treatment

Before coming to see me Karl had seen six or seven other therapists. He had become more deeply involved with two of them than with the others. One was a woman with whom he had accumulated 250 analytic hours at age 20. It seems that this treatment did not succeed. Then at the age of 36, Karl went to see a woman psychotherapist who soon developed breast cancer, but she worked with him until he moved to another city. Two years later he came to see me. The therapist with breast cancer died shortly after we began working together. Because of his previous experiences in therapy, and because of the death of his prior therapist, Karl initially could not develop a therapeutic alliance with me. But even if he had not had his previous aborted therapeutic experiences, because of his background he would still have tried to "control" our relationship.

Initially, Karl used each analytic session with me as if it were a discrete "point" where time stopped and began its journey again. Thus, I could not reach him, just like the arrow that cannot "catch up" with the running man. I became aware of this and I emphasized the need to develop a working alliance rather than "analyzing away" his symptoms. My efforts slowly succeeded, and together we began to understand the nature of his internal world. In the beginning of his third year of analysis, he finally brought a direct representation of his interaction with his early environment to his sessions. The following clinical material comes from this period.

Karl reported having fantasies of defecating on the way to my office. He thought of bringing the feces to me so that I could look at it. The genetic aspect of his fantasy seemed obvious to both of us. I told him that his wish for me to look at his feces might suggest his readiness to examine with me the meanings attached to his feces and its role in his object relations. He accepted that he equated defecating with the reduction of his tensions, but he added that he felt afraid of the dangerous qualities of his feces. He said his feces could kill me. It should be recalled that the therapist whom he saw before me had developed a deadly disease after beginning to work with Karl.

Karl's wish to show me his feces balanced his other desire—to hide it or deny its existence. He began to search for a new living place uncontaminated with "feces"—where the bathroom did not adjoin the bedroom. He wanted to move from one location to another in front of my eyes, so to speak, and he wanted an absolutely clean new location. His childhood escape from one location (East Germany) to another (West Germany) had been infused with his parents'

fears and anxieties, as well as his own unexpressed sadism—
the opportunity to have the policeman catch them. Most likely
Karl's father had hoped to leave behind his internal responses
to Nazis and Communists when he went to West Germany.
Karl recalls having a dream in which his father, wearing an
SS uniform, was walking around in East Germany. If his father had actually done so, he would have been punished. Karl
"knew" his father's anxieties because he had internalized
them. But at the same time, he had also internalized his
mother's desire to stay in the first location. His wish to maintain a self in two locations explained why he would buy two
of each clothing item. The first item he could use, and the
second item he could "lock" away in a closet for future use,
but he would never retrieve it. I told him that his insistence
on finding a clean location to move into attested to his externalized attempt to leave his conflicts behind.

After some searching, Karl found a newly built apartment
for rent which he thought fit his internal requirements. However, while visiting it for a last inspection before signing a
rental contract, he heard water running. Apparently the
sound came from a nearby creek. Hearing this sound caused
his body to react with a stuffed nose and abdominal cramps.
He also had the unusual experience of feeling like a larva, a
trichina, inside a pig's body. Karl told me that a trichina does
not kill the host pig, but it has no way out. When someone
eats the trichinous pig's flesh, however, the larva evolves into
a worm in the new host's body, sucks out all of the new host's
energy, weakens, and finally kills the individual. I told him
that he must have perceived the creek as a very big toilet. His
stuffed nose disallowed him from smelling it, and his abdominal cramps indicated his attempt to rid himself of the anxiety
it produced. Furthermore, the significant noise, that sounded
to him like water running in a toilet, had given him the pes-
simistic notion that he could not, after all, escape from an internalized anxious world, even in a changed location. Since
he had internalized his parents' dangerous "secret" and their

intrusions into his physical and psychological functions when he moved from East Germany to West Germany, he carried his internal burden with him wherever he went. Only through the medium of his obsessive–compulsive symptoms could he maintain the illusion of two separate worlds and the hope that he could escape from a disturbing one to a "clean" one. I told him that behind his obsessive–compulsive symptoms existed his core, filled with "bad" feelings, that stayed with him in every "world," and that I would willingly work with him to modify this core.

Karl responded to my remarks with laughter, which seemed to release his obvious tension. He said that he was laughing at the idea of the creek as a "very big toilet." He relaxed and reported that in his childhood, especially after the birth of his brother, he perceived every smell, every noise, and every movement as dangerous. I explained that feces represented a combination of external (i.e., the mother's intrusion into his bodily and psychic space) and internal (i.e., anal fantasies) dangers for him. After my explanation he reported a dream of being in a train station toilet in which his feces were half in and half out. With a finger he broke off the outside feces, and he now realized that he had found a way to solve his fear of defecating—*he* could master his feces and the function of defecating. For some weeks now he had not paid the debt incurred by his analysis. After reporting this dream he "produced" money (feces) and paid me what he owed me. Soon Karl did move to a new apartment (but not to the one near the creek), and as his analytic sessions continued, we began to unravel the complex structure of his core self representation.

Replacing Body Language with Words

In one of his sessions Karl described an externalized "torture machine." Karl had read about a terrorist organization, the PKK (Kurdish Worker's Party), that had attacked some Turkish institutions located in Germany. The PKK had also threatened some Kurds in Germany (their own ethnic group), and Karl felt that the PKK meant to establish a "torture machine" in Germany. He decided that all PKK Kurds should be driven out of Germany, even though he had empathy for the Kurds living in Turkey, whom he thought were not allowed to speak their own language.

Once more Karl's preoccupation concerned a political conflict and his solution to it consisted of a migration. This matched closely his parents' and ancestors' migrations. I inquired about the terror or the terrorists in himself: his "black thing" which he had recently referred to as a trichina. He had explained, "If the larva gets out of its container, it kills!" I told him that like the PKK terrorists who killed their own people as well as Turks, he might fear that something in his own core could kill *himself* as well as his parents. "You said that the Kurds were not allowed to speak their own language. If you allow yourself to speak *your* own language to express your internal dilemma, you may be able to stop using your body as a spokesperson," I suggested. Karl began to cry, a most unusual response for him up to this time. I felt it was a good sign. Karl was allowing himself to feel emotions pertaining to his helplessness through a *proper* body response: crying.

Karl then reported to me that when he was a child in East Germany, his parents would speak Hungarian, a language he did not understand, whenever they discussed their "secret." Even though they succeeded in preventing him from comprehending their words, they did not prevent him from internalizing their anxiety and their sense of danger. Anna Freud's and Dorothy Burlingham's (1942) study on children in wartime London revealed that if the mothers of these children remained calm during bombing, their offspring would also remain calm. In Karl's situation, his caretakers' anxiety transmitted directly to him. I told him that his insistence on staying "clean" was an attempt to deny his own and his caretakers' anxiety.

When his family left East Germany, they understandably could take only a few possessions with them. They did not know what they might later wish that they had brought, and yet they could not encumber themselves with too many goods either. They wanted to take just those items necessary to make a new start, but often those very items would endanger them by giving away their secret. So whenever Karl had to retrieve *anything* he would feel again his parents' anxieties and tensions, and then he would feel abdominal cramps as if he were trying to get rid of those feelings by defecating. But he did not dare to do so lest by his anal sadism he would destroy his parents and thus render himself completely helpless. After having done a lot of work in our sessions connecting his bodily symptoms with his past, which he had been doomed to remember only bodily, rather than in words, which would have allowed him to process these feelings, he expressed a profound change. He declared that he had realized, while down in the basement, that he could take and return items to the basement anytime, without danger. Subsequent to this realization, his tension lessened; his abdominal cramps and obsessive–compulsive symptoms slowly began to reduce in frequency.

Karl's "Torture Machine"

Once Karl began to give up his obsessive–compulsive symptoms and utilize more appropriate body language, I anticipated seeing more direct expression of his infantile psychotic self in his treatment; if the envelope opens one sees the contents of the envelope! I was not disappointed. When speaking of PKK, he had perceived the group as a "torture machine." Now he felt ready to tell me that he had carried his own "torture machine," externalized, but *within* his psychic space all along. He had "known" that it existed, but he had kept it a secret.

One night while sitting on his bed, it occurred to him that he should pray and thank God. This thought reminded him of his previous preoccupation with religion, the meaning of which we had discussed at some length in treatment. At this time, he also fully sensed his torture machine. He could not see it, but he could "hear" the machine talking to him. "You can't pray sitting on your bed. You should kneel down on the floor," it told him. Karl felt, however, that if he knelt down, "I would lose my true sense of self. However, without my torture machine, I'll be nothing." I surmised that his "mad" core had a parasitic (symbiotic) relationship with the pig-mother. It was saturated with "bad" feelings, such as mother's anxiety, mother's murderous feelings for him, grandmother's intrusion, his helpless rage. The torture machine was a reservoir of his projections of these horrible feelings and his horrible caretakers; but unlike typical projections, which attach to other people or things, Karl's "projections" remained within the psychic space of his core self representation.

The difference between Karl's experience of PKK terrorists as a symbolic reservoir of his inner core and his experience of the "torture machine" within his psychic space needs an explanation. In the first instance, his "envelope self" with its advanced ego functions projected something "bad" he felt inside of him (his infantile psychotic self) onto a suitable symbolic reservoir outside of his psychic space. In the second instance the "projection" took place *within* his infantile psychotic self in a hallucinatory way. This is a difficult concept to describe, since we think of the infantile psychotic self as in an undifferentiated state, which makes the mechanism of *proper* projections infeasible. We need, however, to recall Volkan's (1995) original description of the concept of the infantile psychotic self and the hierarchical aspect of it. He writes:

> The infantile psychotic self may not remain static but grow—assimilating influences and unconscious fantasies related to self- and object images from different phases of childhood—and comes to include identifications with early part-objects while reality testing remains ineffective [p. 60].

Listening to Karl's own description of his inner "torture machine," I surmised that it was a "part object" at the periphery but still within his infantile psychotic self. Therefore, for Karl to submit to his "torture machine" would mean the return of horrible affects directly into the center of his core. On the other hand, I sensed that without the "torture machine" Karl might truly become "nothing." The "torture machine," however unsatisfactorily, provided his infantile psychotic core with some hope for object relations.

One night the "torture machine" spoke to him and said (as his grandmother used to say): "Will has died." As he described this event, he experienced abdominal cramps in the session and wanted to curse. But all he could say was the slang word for a *small* penis. This reflected his infantile helplessness in dealing with the "bad feelings" which saturated his infantile psychotic self. When I explained this to him, he allowed himself to find more suitable expressions for his infantile rage, to replace either letting it saturate his infantile core or projecting it into his "torture machine." In his sessions he slowly began to experience rage against me, a real external object, which led to the fading of his "torture machine." He now used words instead of bodily symptoms to express himself. Initially he feared that I would throw him out of my office. "Immigrants and asylum seekers have to be polite," he would say. (I must add here that Karl never pursued obtaining official German citizenship, even after the political reunification of the two Germanies. He did not "know" whether he was considered Hungarian or German.) He also cried. Once more I considered his tears a sign of his therapeutic progress.

Taming the Crocodile

A few months later, while I was on vacation, Karl did something important. He undertook what Novey (1968) called a "second look." Karl went to the former East German town he had left and looked for his childhood home. He visited the house and spoke with its current occupants. Then he spent a lot of time in a nearby park, where he found a moving mechanical man in the middle of a pond that he remembered visiting as a child. The mechanical man was doing something with his hand, looking at the result, and then shaking his head as if not satisfied with what he had done. The mechanical man, doomed to repeat his own actions, made Karl think, "the 'man' is denying his own self" and his thought made him increasingly tense. He continued to watch with fascination, and realized that furthermore, the "man" had no control over his movements and no autonomy—the pressure of the water moved "his" body. Karl realized that this mechanical man represented himself, whose infant body was directed by his mother. His realization gave him insight into his early experiences on an emotional level. He now sensed that he might join his "two worlds" after all. He also felt that once he accomplished this, he would know that time runs on a continuum, and that this mode of understanding time's flow is not dangerous.

Feeling odd, he continued walking about his old East German town. He came to a beautiful location where the colors of the trees and the light saturated him with "good" feelings. This sense of saturation with "good" feelings seemed to him to have been his goal his whole life. In fact, only through this achievement could he modify his infantile psychotic self (Volkan, 1995). After his "second look" we resumed our work together. Karl felt a change in his attitude toward me, as if I had become a "new object" (Leowald, 1960), a nurturing one. Karl reminded me of an incident that had taken place during the first year of his treatment.

He had brought me a gift. It was a big stuffed toy crocodile, with its mouth wide open and many teeth showing. Karl said that the pink of the mouth looked like a vagina. With its open mouth (a vagina dentata) and its tail (penis), it looked like a greedy bisexual little monster. The crocodile came in a pouch. Karl handed the toy in its pouch to me and said that he wanted me to keep it. At that time I did not have a clear idea of the meaning of the crocodile in a pouch, or of his giving it to me. I told him that we could leave it in my office until we analyzed it. A few days later he took it to his apartment, but he insisted that it belonged to *me*. Slowly I understood that the crocodile in its pouch was an externalized version of his enveloped infantile psychotic self, his envelope equating to the pouch, and his rage-filled "internal nucleus" equating to the many-toothed monster. Later in his development it had also absorbed psychosexual fantasies, that is, fantasies about sadistic feces in the abdomen.

After having his "second look" Karl declared that, after all, the crocodile did not belong to me anymore, he owned it now. He said that he felt like a wild animal, and that I was trying to feed this wild animal. "You don't need to be afraid anymore," he said, "no longer is there danger that I'll bite off your feeding [helping] hand."

Karl and I still have much more work to complete. What I have reported here gives clinical evidence of some of the important concepts examined in this book.

References

Abraham, K. (1924), A short study of the development of the libido, viewed in the light of mental disorders. *Selected Papers on Psychoanalysis.* London: Hogarth Press, pp. 418–501.

Boyer, L. B. (1961), Provisional evaluation of psycho-analysis with few parameters employed in the treatment of schizophrenia. *Internat. J. Psycho-Anal.*, 42:389–403.

———— (1983), *The Regressed Patient.* New York: Jason Aronson.

Freud, A., & Burlingham, D. (1942), *War and Children.* New York: International Universities Press.

Leowald, H. W. (1960), On the therapeutic action of psychoanalysis. *Internat. J. Psycho-Anal.*, 41:16–33.

Novey, S. (1968), *The Second Look: The Reconstruction of Personal History in Psychiatry and Psychoanalysis.* Baltimore: Johns Hopkins University Press.

Volkan, V. D. (1976), *Primitive Internalized Object Relations: A Clinical Study of Schizophrenic, Borderline, and Narcissistic Patients.* New York: International Universities Press.

———— (1995), *Infantile Psychotic Self: Understanding and Treating Schizophrenics and Other Difficult Patients.* Northvale, NJ: Jason Aronson.

7

The Verbal Squiggle Game in Treating the Seriously Disturbed Patient

L. Bryce Boyer, M.D.

During almost half a century of treating seriously regressed patients psychoanalytically, I have become convinced that working through the countertransference is indispensable for a favorable therapeutic outcome.

My training began in the 1940s in an ultraconservative training institute where the psychoanalytic treatment of Freud's "narcissistic neuroses" was strongly disapproved. Only the patient's intrapsychic dynamics were to determine the nature

Acknowledgments: Versions of this communication have been presented at the Seminar for the Advanced Study of the Psychoses, April 14, 1994, San Francisco; the Northern California Society for Psychoanalytic Psychology, May 21, 1994; San Francisco and the Eleventh International Symposium for the Psychotherapy of Schizophrenia, June 15, 1994, Washington, DC.

Deep gratitude is offered to Drs. Thomas H. Ogden and Beatrice Patsalides for their assistance with this manuscript.

and timing of interpretations. As was the custom in North America, Freud's oft-reiterated ambivalence and contradictions concerning the nature and utility of countertransference were essentially ignored (Boyer, 1994); it was seen solely as the therapist's pathological response. Doubting Freud's bases for eschewing such treatment of regressed patients (Boyer, 1967), largely on the basis of lifelong experience with a periodically psychotic mother and lack of success in working in a traditional way with regressed patients, I experimented systematically, despite the heated disapprobation of my mentors (Boyer, 1961, 1966).

In my experiment of using psychoanalysis for the treatment of the seriously disturbed patient, it became apparent soon that the analysand's fears of his aggression constituted a major obstacle. Setting a framework of conditions of therapy, deviations from which were spoken of overtly and promptly and suitably interpreted, assisted in bringing the patient's and analyst's hostility or anxiety about it into focus. This structuring reduced the tendency of both analyst and analysand to express their unconscious thoughts, feelings, impulses, and memories in action. I am more comfortable when the patient's scrutiny does not hinder my access to my own state of reverie (Bion, 1962b); therefore my patients use the couch.

It is now generally agreed that transference–countertransference relations can be studied only in terms of container and contained, and that those relations are much more easily understood and interpretable in the presence of a consistent analytic frame, deviations from which are not ignored (Bion, 1962a,b, 1963, 1987; Modell, 1976). As Ogden (1994) has discussed, the analyst must have the capacity to be aware not only of the patient's transference and simultaneously his own countertransference reactions; in addition he must develop the capacity to allow an analytic (intersubjective) third to be elaborated, understood, and eventually interpreted. I completely agree. Additionally, in my judgment, the maintenance of the analytic frame is *mandatory* for the successful treatment of severely disturbed patients. Other significant contributors to the development of a theory of counter-transference include Winnicott, 1947; Heimann, 1950, 1960; Little, 1951, 1957; Racker, 1952, 1960; Money-Kyrle, 1956; Grinberg, 1957; Bleger, 1962; M. Balint, 1968; Milner, 1969; Meltzer, 1975; Green, 1975; Sandler, 1976; Searles, 1979; Volkan, 1981, 1995; Grotstein, 1981; Ogden, 1982, 1986, 1989; Symington, 1983; Joseph, 1985; Kernberg, 1985; Pick, 1985; Bollas, 1987; Giovacchini, 1989; Tansey and Burke, 1989; McLaughlin, 1991; Etchegoyen, 1991; Gabbard, 1991; Jacobs, 1991; Blechner, 1992; D. Rosenfeld, 1992; E. Balint, 1993; Steiner, 1993; Pallaro, 1994.

Probably as a result of child analysis and the heightened use of psychoanalytic psychotherapy for severe character-ological, narcissistic and borderline disorders, and psychotic disturbances, as well as psychosomatic and alexithymic disorders, the crucial importance of the way in which the therapist uses his own conscious and unconscious responses to the patient, whether psychical, somatic, verbal, or nonverbal, has now been more clearly recognized (Etchegoyen, 1991; Boyer, 1994).

In the course of the past thirty years a change has occurred in our understanding of the analytic task: "It is now widely held that, instead of being about the patient's intrapsychic dynamics, interpretation should be made about *the interaction* of patient and analyst *at an intrapsychic level*" (O'Shaughnessy, 1983, p. 281).

Definition of a Countertransference

The concept of transference-countertransference as I use it follows H. A. Rosenfeld's (1987) contribution, detailing the constant, principally unconscious interplay between analyst and analysand involving their mutual introjection of the other's projective identifications. Regarding counter-transference, projective identification functions as a means of communication by which the analyst learns from the patient what the latter cannot think consciously. Within the field of the "analytic third" (constituted by the interaction between patient and analyst at an intrapsychic level), the analyst seeks and "finds" (in the Winnicottian sense of "finding an object," that is, playfully creating) words to bridge the subjective states of the analyst and the patient, while understanding the paradox that the psychological space that *separates* them constitutes at the same time the potentially powerful *link* that *connects* the patient's dissociated states (Bion, 1959; Volkan, 1981).

Poggi (personal communication, 1995) notes:

> Part of the countertransference experience with certain patients is a sharing of body boundary confusion that, for a time, leaves me uncertain of my own sensation and therefore of my own distinct physical response to the presence of the patient. A good deal of what is ultimately imagined in the course of such a countertransference experience is built on these now confused sensations.

What follows briefly mentions some aspects of working through the countertransference that have seemed to be particularly important.

Working Through the Countertransference: The Analyst's Personal Experiences

It is my view that whatever the analyst experiences during the analytic session is influenced heavily by his idiosyncratic introjection and reformulation of the patient's verbal and nonverbal communications, containing the patient's projections. We should not be misled into thinking our stray, apparently unrelated thoughts, fantasies, physical, or emotional reactions can be dismissed as idle preoccupations, taking us away from the business at hand, interfering with our free-floating or evenly hovering attention (Boyer and Doty, 1993).

Cultural Influences on the Analyst's Experiences

However, I do not infer that everything the analyst thinks or feels should be considered countertransference. It is clear that factors other than introjection of the patient's projections are significantly operative in the analyst's perceptions of his patient's communications. The analyst's prevailing emotional state and individual conflicts, repressed or otherwise, will determine his degree of openness to the patient's communications.

The mental set of the analyst is firmly embedded in his cultural life history with its unconscious biases that strongly influence his receptivity. For example, my lifelong experiences with psychotic people have conditioned me to be *automatically* aware of very early stages of regression as possibly premonitory of a psychotic outbreak. For example, when a patient who customarily uses correct grammar begins to misuse the pronouns "I" and "me," I am alerted to the possibility that the analysand is on the verge of a regression to the developmental stage when he was unsure whether he was "I" or "me" (E. Balint, 1993).

My research in anthropology and study of folklore and the cross-cultural use of the Rorschach Test (Boyer, 1979, 1995; L. B. Boyer, R. M. Boyer, Dithrich, Harned, Hippler, Stone, and Walt, 1989; DeVos and Boyer, 1989) have led me, in agreement with Freud (1900), to believe firmly that each symbol has at least one basic meaning, apparently inborn, in addition to whatever other meanings that have been added subsequently. As an example: in a session an adolescent boy entered an acute psychotic regression during which words and eventually their syllables became concrete objects for him. As he began to pound violently on a desk, he shouted repeatedly first "table" and then, frantically, "ta"—"bul," "ta"—"bul." My automatic recollection of Freud's use of both wood and table as symbols for female or mother enabled me to say that I thought he feared he had destroyed his mother and wanted help in reconstituting her. The psychotic regression immediately disappeared (Boyer, 1972). That the interpretation was so effective, depended on the nature of the transference–countertransference interaction, in which I was then solidly a benevolent paternal figure, whom he understood to be giving him permission to possess some of the love of his mother. When the interpretation of the symbology was made, however, this important element of my countertransference formed an unconscious background to our interaction. Further, I was simultaneously experiencing at a subliminal level my analysand's pain and despair, while detachedly observing not only his actions and emotions, but my own (see Ogden, 1994).

Automatically thinking of problems related to unresolved sibling rivalry when patients begin to talk of tiny animals or insects (Boyer, 1979), or Christmas (Boyer, 1955), or Easter (Boyer, 1985) often leads to a quickened introjection and understanding of a projection. A patient expressed himself in a boring manner for many months (Boyer and Doty, 1993); he had never mentioned music. Once while drowsy, I became aware of hearing humming and vague melodies, although there was utter silence in the room. My inquiry whether he were listening to music led to his revealing he had done so throughout his time with me when on the couch. Our subsequent learning that music for him symbolized the umbilical cord and the inspiration of air was a significant turning point of his analysis.

The Verbal Squiggle Game

Observing that analysands often continue symbolically the themes of one interview to the next, led me to seek to view each analytic session as though it were a dream, in which the major unresolved transference–countertransference issue of the last or last few sessions composes the "day residue" (Boyer, 1988). I now assume that *every* communication of the interview very likely may in some way be related to that day residue in the context of the ensuing "dream" and am particularly interested in the symbolic meanings of the opening verbal or nonverbal communications. I believe that viewing the interview as if it were a dream serves as a part of, leads to the background for, or constitutes a part of the verbal squiggle game, in which the analyst is prepared to enter a mild reverie. Occasionally, as a session opens, analysands visualize events from the previous meeting as "scenes" on a wall or an imaginary movie screen (Lewin, 1948).

My usual technical orientation involves my seeking to be, in the words of E. Balint (1993), "quiet and nonintrusive, but also absolutely *there*," while "the patient is occupied in finding his own words or actions" (p. 4). The length of the period during which I remain this relatively passive while receiving stimuli actively through all my senses, depends on the capacity of the patient to accept and use profitably my tentative interpretations. This state rarely lasts longer than a few months, at the end of which time I usually feel quite relaxed in the presence of my analysand and frequently find myself in a light trance during which fantasies and primary process thinking are often intermixed with my more customary social thinking.

As I find myself progressively both more at ease and able to associate more freely, I usually find myself anxiety-free as I offer trial interpretations to be considered by the analysand. I wait less long for the analysand to recall formerly offered material inconsistent with present data and more actively suggest that the patient's conflictual or genetic explanations of anxiety might be modified by alternate explanations. As we become more accustomed to one another, in my role as analytic third I am aware that my introjections are not infrequently psychosomatic: a tightness in the chest, muscle group tensions, abdominal cramps, barely perceptible odors or tastes, transient, vague, visual phenomena. I assume that they reflect the preverbal or presymbolic nature of the patient's unconscious communication of his anxiety. Further, I become more trusting that my perceptions accurately reflect the patient's unconscious projections and feel freer to interpret on the basis of my countertransference reactions. My notion is that at times when the patient and I are (in varying degrees) simultaneously comfortably regressed, we both enter a sort of recapitulation of the hypothetical symbiotic phase of the mother–infant dual unity (Benedek, 1949; Loewald, 1980; Mahler and McDevitt, 1982).

Winnicott (1958, 1965) has stressed the need of the analyst to be able to allow the existence of potential space in which creativity can occur, and Bion (1987) the need for the analyst to enter into a "reverie," allowing a similar development. I find my most exhilarating and productive periods when working with regressed patients to occur during those unusual occasions when, while in the state of reverie to which I believe Bion refers, I quite comfortably and spontaneously play what I conceive to be a verbal version of Winnicott's (1971, pp. 121–123) "squiggle game" with the patient. At such times, the analysand and I have become subjective objects to one another. We do not then use pencils but instead create our "drawings" verbally when the patient's and therapist's associations are obviously contaminated by one another. Then they meet in that potential space in which creativity can occur, enacting an intensification of a verbal squiggle game (see also Deri, 1984, pp. 340–341; Grolnick, 1990, p. 159).

Clinical Illustration

During the verbal squiggle game the thinking of both analysand and analyst can most flexibly and cogently switch, without conflict, to the uses of autistic–contiguous (Ogden, 1989), paranoid–schizoid, and depressive modes of generating experience. It is most doubtful that such an interchange could take place in a therapeutic endeavor in which the analytic frame had not been consistently maintained, or in which the therapist was uncomfortable during the patient's sometimes

psychotic regressions (presumably because of anxiety concerning the analyst's own aggressive or libidinal urges, his
anxiety concerning his own sanity, his capacity to maintain the
analytic frame, and so on).

I record extensive process notes during interviews; in my
notes I seek to include my own fantasies, physical sensations,
and emotional changes. The clinical example that follows is
not literally accurate because it is partially reconstructed.

This reported event is unusual in that it *heralded* a salutary
regression during which crucial new information emerged.
In the service of time and space, the report, which was quite
repetitious, is abbreviated greatly.

Dr. M was a middle-aged psychoanalyst whose three previous analyses had not helped him stop acting out sexually with
his clients. During the third year of his treatment with me,
he was able to regress sufficiently to be able to recover memories he validated subsequently as portraying actual events in
his life. The introductions to the memories were recovered
during an interview in which for the first time we played the
verbal squiggle game, a spontaneous activity which surprised
us only retrospectively, even though his interviews were customarily characterized by emotional flatness and heightened
intellectualization. He had never mentioned fairy tales, folklore, or an interest in anthropology. He learned consciously
of my concern with them when he read many of my writings,
beginning some months after our first episode of playing the
squiggle game.

He customarily entered the consultation room moving
briskly and looking hyperalert. Nevertheless, Dr. M never appeared to be aware of any of the room's contents, noting rarely
and only in passing, changes in my facial expressions, dress,
or moods, and never revealing his fantasies concerning them,
either spontaneously or when questioned. No stable transference relationship had developed. For brief periods I appeared
to be the cold, potentially undependable phallic mother of a
preoedipal boy whose rare apparent kindness would lead to

her suddenly and unexpectedly physically hurting him for vaguely defined pleasures of her own, often associated with bathroom activities. At others I seemed to represent the violent, morally weak, sexually exhibitionistic, paranoid, greedy father who beat his young children during temper tantrums, the cause of which were ascribed by Dr. M to his father's being cheated in business, probably by Nazi agents. Ordinarily, I seemed to be solely an impersonal colleague.

Some months before the interview to be reported I had redecorated the consultation room, changing the decor to African, using colorful textiles and ebony statuary. At the foot of the couch was the figure of a seated man holding a large musical instrument on his lap, reaching around it to the strings. The top of the instrument consisted of a head facing forward. The head was almost identical to, but slightly smaller than that of the man, and barely beneath it. Although Dr. M seemed unaware of the changed appearance of the room, during the interview he remarked, without affect or apparent connection to other thoughts, that he had read that aboriginal women sometimes had retractable dentate penises in their vaginas. Some sessions later he mentioned, apparently totally out of context and without connection to any other verbal material or discernible event or curiosity, that as a young boy he once wondered whether a discoloration on the bathroom wall were blood. During some six subsequent months, there was neither further mention of that theme nor reference to the room's decorations.

The day before the session to be described, Dr. M had reported a fragment of a dream in which the vague, immobile figure of a man reminded him of an infamous and widely known effeminate polo player of whom he had recently read, seated on a horse. The polo player was reputed to be cruel to the mounts he rode by choice, sometimes beating or poking them with his mallet. No action occurred in the dream, which was related without emotion or curiosity. I felt certain that the dream depicted symbolically the nature of the dominant transference situation of the previous session, apparently shaped by a fear that as a phallic mother I would use him for my own gratifications. I wondered silently whether the dream was a manifestation of a screen memory of early life events, involving disappointment, sadism, and betrayal in a bedroom setting, because of the inferred horseback riding and the cruelty of the polo player.

The patient's appearance and attitude as he entered the consultation room for his next session were unprecedented. In contrast with his usual brisk motions, hypervigilant, rigid pose on the couch, and matter-of-fact speech, on this day Dr. M came in looking as though he were not yet fully awake, and seemed to float to the couch, where he lay relaxed and silent, and, for the first time, appeared to be in a light trance. I felt myself also entering an altered ego state, and found myself feeling psychologically split, observing him, myself, and our intersubjectivity detachedly, while being simultaneously deeply involved. I revisualized his dream and silently thought he would talk of the statue and turn to passive homosexual fears.

After a time he said he had just noticed the statue for the first time and wondered whether it were of a mother and her son. She seemed to be holding him too intimately and trying to bring his "bottom" closer to her "pelvis."

I heard myself saying, "perhaps to touch his bottom with the penis that can come out?" Unsurprised and clearly pleased, he immediately responded:

Dr. M: "The phallic witch was going to eat Hansel and Gretel but they pushed her into the oven."

Analyst: "Then she couldn't eat them or use the dentate phallus."

Dr. M: "No." He fell silent and dreamily looked about the room, eventually asking whether the previously unmentioned colorful textiles were newly there. After further silence, he continued: "There was blood on the wall of the bedroom and I was so terrified I couldn't think or move."

Analyst: "Several months ago you mentioned wondering whether a discoloration on the *bathroom* wall were blood." He became silent, seemed bewildered, lifted his hands in a gesture of self-protection, and spoke what sounded like mumbled Yiddish. I felt distinctly eerie, and wondered silently whether he would imagine that a man were threatening to enter the room through the closed and locked door at his feet. After a few moments of silence, Dr. M said he had thought he had seen a man's shadow on the closed door at his feet (see Freud [1899, 1904, 1922, 1933]; Devereux [1953]; Major [1983]; Zwiebel [1977, 1984] about the presence of telepathy in psychoanalysis, and its part in occasional countertransference reactions).

Analyst: "When you were mumbling, I thought I heard you say *golem* and *dybbuk.*"

Dr. M: "Yes, I thought I did, too, although I don't think I know what those words mean, except that I think they pertain to dead people."[1]

I commented that he had never spoken Yiddish previously in my presence. He was unsurprised and said he thought he had forgotten that childhood language. After a long, contemplative silence, he continued, "It's my uncle. He's coming through the door and I'm glad to see him, especially because my mother is angry with me and hurting me." Dr. M did not amplify. "He was nice to me when he visited, holding me. I think I never saw him after I was about 7."

Analyst: "He held you in his lap after mother hurt you?"

Becoming alert, Dr. M said, "I didn't know then that he was a *golem* or a *dybbuk*. I only learned that when studying for my bar mitzvah, and reading assigned literature. When I was 4 or 5, he used to lie on the bed with me and hold me." Reentering his trance, he continued: "I feel warm and comforted and loved. I don't mind when he hurts my little asshole with his big cock, I just want to please him."

---

[1] I had an imprecise understanding of the words *golem* and *dybbuk* only because some months previously I had been editing an article on ancient Jewish folklore in conjunction with other work.

Regaining alertness, he continued: "It's only later that I know that he's just using me as a thing and have to become catatonic."

It is impossible, I think, to judge the degree of transferential compliance with my unconscious wish. Three previous patients had seen the ebony figure as two men in sexual relationships. That I was unaware of a wish that Dr. M would join them in his idiosyncratic use of the statue, does not, of course, mean that such a wish was absent. His compliance with his uncle's wish could well have been recapitulated in the transference.

This condensed episode of the squiggle game was the first and most dramatic of several during the three ensuing years of his analysis. It provided the first revelation that Dr. M had suffered a childhood psychosis which he subsequently relived for months in the consultation room. During regressive episodes, Dr. M did indeed relive in the transference–countertransference relationship catatoniclike regressions which recapitulated actual and symbolized psychotic experiences of his boyhood, which had occurred between perhaps 3 and 10 years of age. The details recapitulated his being at times convinced that I was one of his parents or a golem or a dybbuk. Such regressed episodes were limited to periods when he was in the consultation room. They closely resembled forgotten episodes during his early grammar school years when he was under psychiatric care and hospitalized briefly.

For some days at a time, while regressed into a mild form of waxy flexibility, he spoke of the man in the transitory hallucination of his uncle coming through the doorway as a previously "unremembered" uncle whom his parents had act as baby-sitter for Dr. M from ages 3 to 7. He never remembered exactly when or how he learned that his uncle, to his parents' knowledge, had been a convicted pederast.

Analysis of aspects of his perceptions and experiences during his "squiggle games" continued until the end of his analysis. The blood which had been visualized initially as on the bedroom wall was identified eventually as being spots on menstrual rags which had been thrown against the bathroom wall, but displaced in the vision to the bedroom, probably because of his earlier conviction that mother bled after being injured by the father's "mallet" and by his own body, during his birth.

Gradually, during various ensuing regressive episodes which included delusions of being possessed by, or himself an automaton, he reread Jewish folklore and remembered that he had learned about golems and dybbuks in Hebrew school. He brought examples of the folklore literature to interviews and read aloud that dybbuk refers to "an evil spirit possessing man, or the soul of a dead person residing in another's body and acting through it," and that, conversely, golem both represented the shapeless stage of Adam or an embryo, and an artificial man, an automaton (Neilson, Knott and Carhart, 1949, pp. 722, 1076). He also brought other references to the consultation room, some written in Hebrew (Ginsburg, 1913; Dan, 1970). Dr. M recalled that in his early childhood he had been singularly frightened after having heard a recitation of Hansel and Gretel (Grimm and Grimm, 1819), being concerned with the themes of being deserted by his parents and cannibalism.

Discussion

In this presentation and elsewhere (Boyer, 1977, 1978, 1982, 1983, 1986, 1989, 1993, 1994) I have offered examples of the ways in which analyzing countertransference experience has had salutary effects during the analyses of regressed patients. Here I further the discussion of work within the countertransference by describing an example of a verbal squiggle game. In such intersubjective play between analyst and analysand, a generative space is available to each through which new understanding and conceptualizations can emerge, the creativity to which Winnicott often refers. I believe this space to be the most powerful link between the patient's dissociated states (see also H. A. Rosenfeld, 1952).

Such space exists, when it does, through the efforts of the analyst who, within a reverie, adapts himself to the task of attending to both subjective and intersubjective experience. This vital splitting of experience on the part of the analyst is essential to the process of intersubjectivity within the analytic hour, and the sine qua non of the interpretation not only of countertransference material but *through* the countertransference. Accurate interpretation through the countertransference gives lease to a play space through which the analysand, in both his separateness and within the analytic third, newly and creatively expresses his experience.

During such episodes of play, the space's potential for linking dissociated aspects of the analysand's experience is potentiated. I believe that the new connections between previously dissociated states depends on the analyst's ability to tolerate such a type of splitting within himself.

To tolerate such internal flexibility the analyst himself must have been well analyzed by an analyst who was capable of tolerating deep regressive episodes undergone by his patients during their analyses (Racker, 1958). An analyst who does not enable his patient to live through deep regressions during treatment cannot have developed the capacity to experience the inevitable reciprocal countertransference and to learn to use it in the service of treatment, or to teach his analytic trainees. Also, it is possible, although I consider it to be unlikely, that the life experiences of the analyst may have to have been exceptional and his neurophysiological endowments may need to be of a nature that permits special sensitivities. Those sensitivities allow him to experience without great conflict and work through the countertransference he experiences while analyzing such regressions.

It is difficult to tolerate this kind of splitting, particularly to admit the highly personal, private, and embarrassingly mundane aspects of one's subjective experience (Ogden, 1994).

Beyond this, such experiences can be felt as a threat to one's sense of lucidity. At times, one must permit links to fall away, in order to perceive the greater trail of the chain: madness may be experienced in fantasy or body.

Equally important as interpretations made through the countertransference, are the tolerance and containment of this splitting process. We cannot value too highly the patient's introjection of an analytic object of equanimity, which so clearly rests on the capacity for integration of part object, whole object relatedness, the capacity for concern, and a sense of optimism. It must not be forgotten that patients who suffer from Freud's narcissistic neuroses frequently, if not always, have not developed a well-grounded sense of self. This sense of self will arise through the gradual internalization and maturation of the object relationships developed with the analyst during the course of analysis; we can think of Mahler's (1968) "vicissitudes of individuation."

I would like to expand the idea that each interview may be viewed as a dream. As all communications (of both analyst and analysand) are in some way related to the day residue of the enduring "dream," it can be most fruitful for the analyst to apply the tenets of dream analysis to the flow of associations obtained through attention to the subjective–intersubjective process.

Summary

It is proposed in this communication that successful psychotherapeutic work with severely disturbed patients necessitates an intensification of the analyst's attention to his intrapsychic, countertransference experiences stemming from his conscious and unconscious interactions with his patient. The countertransference reactions manifest themselves as psychical, emotional, and somatosensory perceptions. The effectiveness of the analyst's work is heightened by his formulating his interpretations on the basis of those intrapsychic experiences.

Interpreting *through* the countertransference implies the analyst's ability to tolerate a psychic split, simultaneously thinking for himself while with the analysand. During temporary regressions to presymbolic modes of experience that allow for the retrieval and exchange between analyst and analysand of primary process-related fantasies in verbal forms of Winnicott's "squiggle game," the analyst must also be capable of concurrently maintaining an observing ego stance that is informed by secondary process thinking.

Case material demonstrates how countertransference informed interpretations foster the disturbed patient's engagement in the therapeutic process and help him recover repressed memories of early infantile psychic trauma. Through the analyst's complementary regression to and simultaneous interpretation of the analysand's autistic–contiguous and schizoparanoid modes of experience, the patient is enabled to introject the analytic object. This introjection allows for the patient's concurrent experience and integration of part object and whole object relatedness, which, in turn, contributes to the development of a stable sense of self.

Interpreting through the countertransference implies not only that the analyst has worked through primitive mental states during his own training analysis, but that he also works strictly within the analytic frame. Maintaining the frame is essential for the analysis of the patient's hostility, anxiety, and defense mechanisms and materially reduces the probability of the patient's and the analyst's acting out and acting in.

References

Balint, E. (1993), *Before I Was I: Psychoanalysis and the Imagination*, ed. J. L. Mitchell & M. Parsons. New York: Guilford.
Balint, M. (1968), *The Basic Fault*. London: Tavistock.
Benedek, T. (1949), The psychosomatic implications of the primary unit: Mother-Child. *Amer. J. Orthopsychiatry*, 19:642–654.
Bion, W. R. (1959), Attacks on linking. *Internat. J. Psycho-Anal.*, 40:308–315.
———— (1962a), *Learning from Experience*. New York: Basic Books.
———— (1962b), *Second Thoughts*. New York: Jason Aronson.

———— (1963), Elements of psycho-analysis. In: *Seven Servents.* New York: Jason Aronson, 1977.

———— (1987), *Clinical Seminars, Brasilia and Sao Paulo,* ed. F. Bion. Abingdon, U.K.: Fleetwood Press.

Blechner, M. (1992), Working in the countertransference. *Psychoanal. Dialog.,* 2:161–179.

Bleger, J. (1962), Modalidades de la relacion objectal. *Revista de Psicoanalisis,* 19:1–2.

Bollas, C. (1987), *The Shadow of the Object. Psychoanalysis of the Unknown Known.* New York: Columbia University Press.

Boyer, L. B. (1955), Christmas "neurosis." *J. Amer. Psychoanal. Assn.,* 3:467–488.

———— (1961), Provisional evaluation of psychoanalysis with few parameters employed in the treatment of schizophrenia. *Internat. J. Psycho-Anal.,* 42:389–403.

———— (1966), Office treatment of schizophrenic patients by psychoanalysis. *Psychoanal. Forum,* 1:337–356.

———— (1967), Historical development of psychoanalytic psychotherapy of the schizophrenias: Freud's contributions. In: *Psychoanalytic Treatment of Schizophrenic and Characterological Disorders,* ed. L. B. Boyer & P. L. Giovacchini. New York: Science House Press.

———— (1972), A suicidal attempt by an adolescent twin. *Internat. J. Psychoanal. Psychother.,* 1:7–30.

———— (1977), Working with a borderline patient. *Psychoanal. Quart.,* 46:386–424.

———— (1978), Countertransference experiences in working with severely regressed patients. *Contemp. Psychoanal.,* 14:48–72.

———— (1979), *Childhood and Folklore. A Psychoanalytic Study of Apache Personality.* New York: Library of Psychological Anthropology.

———— (1982), Analytic experiences in work with regressed patients. In: *Technical Factors in the Treatment of the Severely Disturbed Patient,* ed. P. L. Giovacchini & L. B. Boyer. New York: Jason Aronson, pp. 65–106.

———— (1983), *The Regressed Patient.* New York: Jason Aronson.

———— (1985), Christmas "neurosis" reconsidered. In: *Depressive States and Their Treatment,* ed. V. D. Volkan. Northvale, NJ: Jason Aronson, pp. 297–316.

———— (1986), Technical aspects of treating the regressed patient. *Contemp. Psychoanal.,* 22:25–44.

———— (1988), Thinking of the interview as though it were a dream. *Contemp. Psychoanal.,* 24:275–281.

———— (1989), Countertransference and technique in working with the regressed patient. Further remarks. *Internat. J. Psycho-Anal.,* 70:701–714.

———— (1992), Roles played by music as revealed through countertransference facilitated regression. *Internat. J. Psycho-Anal.,* 73:55–70.

———— (1993), Introduction: Countertransference—Brief history and clinical issues with regressed patients. In: *Master Clinicians on Treating the*

Regressed Patient, Vol. 2, ed. L. B. Boyer & P. L. Giovacchini. Northvale, NJ: Jason Aronson, pp. 1–22.

—— (1994), Countertransference: Condensed history and personal view of issues with regressed patients. *J. Psychother. Pract. & Res.*, 3:122–137.

—— (1995), *A Selection of Cross-Cultural Studies Using the Rorschach Test: 1961–1994.* Berkeley, CA: Boyer Research Institute.

—— Boyer, R. M., Dithrich, C. W., Harned, H., Hippler, A. E., Stone, J. S., & Walt, A. (1989), The relation between psychological states and acculturation among the Tanana and Upper Tanana Indians of Alaska. *Ethos*, 17:387–427.

—— Doty, L. (1993), Countertransference, regression and an analysand's uses of music. In: *Master Clinicians on Treating the Regressed Patient*, Vol. 2, ed. L. B. Boyer & P. L. Giovacchini. Northvale, NJ: Jason Aronson, pp. 173–204.

Dan, Y. (1970), Maggid (in Hebrew). *Encyclopedia Hebraica*, 22:139–140.

Deri, S. (1984), *Symbolization and Creativity.* New York: International Universities Press.

Devereux, G. (1953), *Psychoanalysis and the Occult.* New York: International Universities Press.

DeVos, G. A., & Boyer, L. B. (1989), *Symbolic Analysis Cross-Culturally.* Berkeley, CA: University of California Press.

Etchegoyen, R. H. (1991), *The Fundamentals of Psychoanalytic Technique.* London: Karnac.

Freud, S. (1899), A premonitory dream fulfilled. *Standard Edition*, 5:623–625. London: Hogarth Press, 1953.

—— (1900), The Interpretation of Dreams. *Standard Edition*, 4 & 5. London: Hogarth Press, 1953.

—— (1904), Premonitions and chance: An excerpt. In: *Psychoanalysis and the Occult,* ed. G. Devereux. New York: International Universities Press, pp. 52–55, 1963.

—— (1922), Dreams and telepathy. *Standard Edition*, 18:195–220. London: Hogarth Press, 1955.

—— (1933), Dreams and occultism. *Standard Edition*, 22:31–56. London: Hogarth Press, 1964.

Gabbard, G. O. (1991), Technical approaches to transference hate in the analysis of borderline patients. *Internat. J. Psycho-Anal.*, 76:625–638.

Ginsburg, L. (1913), *The Legends of the Jews,* Vol. 4. Philadelphia, PA: The Jewish Publication Society of America.

Giovacchini, P. L. (1989), *Countertransference Triumphs and Catastrophes.* Northvale, NJ: Jason Aronson.

Green, A. (1975), The analyst, symbolization and absence in the analytic setting. (On changes in analytic practice and analytic experience.) *Internat. J. Psycho-Anal.*, 60:347–356.

Grimm, J., & Grimm, W. (1819), *Grimm's Fairy Tales for Young and Old. The Complete Stories,* tr. R. Mannheim. Garden City, NY: Doubleday, 1977.

Grinberg, L. (1957), Perturbaciones en la interpretacion por la contra-identificacion proyectiva. *Revista de Psicoanalisis*, 14:23–28.

Grolnick, S. (1990), *The Work and Play of Winnicott*. Northvale, NJ: Jason Aronson.

Grotstein, J. S. (1981), *Splitting and Projective Identification*. New York: Jason Aronson.

Heimann, P. (1950), Countertransference. *Internat. J. Psycho-Anal.*, 31:81–84.

———— (1960), Countertransference. *Brit. J. Med. Psychol.*, 33:9–15.

Jacobs, T. (1991), *The Use of the Self Countertransference and Communication in the Analytic Setting*. Madison, CT: International Universities Press.

Joseph, B. (1985), Transference: The total situation. *Internat. J. Psycho-Anal.*, 66:47–54.

Kernberg, O. F. (1985), *Internal World and External Reality*. Northvale, NJ: Jason Aronson.

Lewin, B. D. (1948), Inferences from the dream screen. *Internat. J. Psycho-Anal.*, 29:224–231.

Little, M. I. (1951), Countertransference and the patient's response to it. In: *Transference Neurosis and Transference Psychosis*. New York: Jason Aronson, pp. 35–50.

———— (1957), "R"—the analyst's total response to his patient's needs. In: *Transference Neurosis and Transference Psychosis*. New York: Jason Aronson, pp. 51–80.

Loewald, H. (1980), *Papers on Psychoanalysis*. New Haven, CT: Yale University Press.

Mahler, M. S. (1968), *On Human Symbiosis and the Vicissitudes of Individuation*. New York: International Universities Press.

Mahler, M. S., & McDevitt, J. B. (1982), Thoughts on emergence of the sense of self, with particular emphasis on the body self. *J. Amer. Psychoanal. Assn.*, 30:827–848.

Major, R., ed. (1983), *Confrontation: Telepathie*, Vol. 10. Paris: Aubier-Montaigne.

McLaughlin, J. (1991), Clinical and theoretic aspects of enactment. *J. Amer. Psychoanal. Assn.*, 39:595–614.

Meltzer, D. (1975), Adhesive identification. *Contemp. Psychoanal.*, 11:289–310.

Milner, M. (1969), *The Hands of the Living God*. London: Hogarth Press.

Modell, A. (1976), "The holding environment" and the therapeutic action of psychoanalysis. *J. Amer. Psychoanal. Assn.*, 24:285–308.

Money-Kyrle, R. (1956), Normal countertransference and some of its deviations. *Internat. J. Psycho-Anal.*, 37:360–366.

Neilson, W. A., Knott, T. A., & Carhart, P. W., Eds. (1949), *Webster's New International Dictionary of the English Language*. 2nd ed., unabridged. Springfield, MA: G. & C. Merriam.

Ogden, T. H. (1982), *Projective Identification and Psychotherapeutic Technique*. New York: Jason Aronson.

———— (1986), *The Matrix of the Mind. Object Relations and the Psychoanalytic Technique*. New York: Jason Aronson.

———— (1989), *The Primitive Edge of Experience*. Northvale, NJ: Jason Aronson.

———— (1994), Projective identification and the subjugating third. In: *Subjects of Analysis*. Northvale, NJ: Jason Aronson, pp. 97–106.

O'Shaughnessy, E. (1983), Words and working through. *Internat. J. Psycho-Anal.*, 64:281–290.

Pallaro, P. (1994), Somatic countertransference: The therapist in relationship. Paper presented at the Third European Arts Therapies Conference. Ferrara, Italy, September.

Pick, I. (1985), Working through in the countertransference. In: *Melanie Klein Today. Volume II. Mainly Practice*, ed. E. Spillius. London: Routledge, 1988, pp. 34–47.

Racker, E. (1952), Observaciones sobre la contratransferencia como instrumento tecnico; comunicacion preliminar. *Revista de Psicoanalisis*, 9:342–354.

———— (1958), Classical and present techniques in psychoanalysis. In: *Transference and Countertransference*. New York: International Universities Press, 1960, pp. 23–70.

———— (1960), Study of early conflicts by relation to interpretation. *Internat. J. Psycho-Anal.*, 41:47–58.

Rosenfeld, D. (1992), Countertransference and the psychotic part of the personality. In: *The Psychotic Part of the Personality*. London: Karnac, pp. 79–100.

Rosenfeld, H. A. (1952), Notes on the psychoanalysis of confusional states in chronic schizophrenia. *Internat. J. Psycho-Anal.*, 31:132–137.

———— (1987), *Impasse and Interpretation*. London: Tavistock.

Sandler, J. (1976), Countertransference and role responsiveness. *Internat. Rev. Psycho-Anal.*, 3:43–47.

Searles, H. (1979), *Countertransference and Related Subjects*. New York: International Universities Press.

Steiner, J. (1993), *Psychic Retreats. Pathological Organizations in Psychotic Neurotic and Borderline Patients*. London: Routledge.

Symington, N. (1983), The analyst's act of freedom as agent of therapeutic change. *Internat. Rev. Psycho-Anal.*, 10:283–291.

Tansey, M., & Burke, W. (1989), *Understanding Countertransference: From Projective Identification to Empathy*. Hillsdale, NJ: Analytic Press.

Volkan, V. D. (1981), *Linking Objects and Linking Phenomena*. New York: International Universities Press.

———— (1995), *The Infantile Psychotic Self and Its Fates*. Northvale, NJ: Jason Aronson.

Winnicott, D. W. (1947), Hate in the countertransference. *Collected Papers: Through Paediatrics to Psycho-Analysis*. New York: Basic Books, 1958, pp. 194–203.

———— (1958), *Collected Papers: Through Paediatrics to Psycho-Analysis*. New York: Basic Books.

———— (1965), *The Maturational Processes and the Facilitating Environment*. New York: International Universities Press.

———— (1971), *Playing and Reality*. New York: International Universities Press.

Zwiebel, R. (1977), Der Analytiker Traumt von seinem Patientin. *Psyche*, 31:43–59.

———— (1984), Zur Dynamik des Gegenubertragunstraums. *Psyche*, 38:193–213.

Part Three

Summarizing Reflections

8

Constitution, Environment, and Fantasy in the Organization of the Psychotic Core

Salman Akhtar, M.D.

Introducing an element of play in an otherwise grim subject, Volkan and I decided to adapt the two parts of our book's title as the individual titles of our opening and concluding chapters. This bifurcation of the book's title yielded the titles of Volkan's chapter ("The Seed of Madness") and that of my chapter ("Constitution, Environment, and Fantasy in the Organization of the Psychotic Core"). In keeping with the spirit of a subtitle, which explains, elucidates, and elaborates upon the title, my chapter will be a conceptual follow-up on ideas contained in Volkan's chapter. However, I will also refer to the other chapters in this volume, bring in significant contributions from beyond this book's confines, and voice my own opinions. Remaining faithful to the title of my chapter, I will divide its contents into three sections, separated largely for didactic purposes: (1) hereditary and constitutional factors; (2) the environmental contribution; and (3) the role of fantasy. After covering these three areas, I will make concluding remarks which will summarize the preceding ideas and highlight their significance for the treatment of psychotic and potentially psychotic individuals.

Hereditary and Constitutional Factors

From all external appearances, it seems that a hereditary factor in the etiology of schizophrenia and its related forms of psychopathology has been sufficiently illustrated. Many types of evidence support this claim. These include the higher incidence of schizophrenia among the relatives of probands (Rosenthal, 1975), the greater concordance rates among monozygotic than in dizygotic twins (Gottesman and Shields, 1966; Kringlen, 1967; Tienari, 1968, 1991), and most impressively, the persistence of a high vulnerability to the illness in identical twins reared apart from birth onwards (Kety, Rosenthal, Wender, and Schulsinger, 1968, 1971, 1975; Wender, Rosenthal, Kety, Schulsinger, and Welner, 1974). While impressive, this line of thinking is not devoid of pitfalls. To begin with, diagnostic uncertainties and disagreements plague the epidemiologic statistical studies in this area. Moreover, the increasingly narrow definition of schizophrenia in the current nosological systems tends to eliminate milder and nonpsychotic forms of the malady (Kernberg, 1984; Akhtar, 1992a) from such investigations. Among other difficulties is the problem of distinguishing cause and effect in this realm. While constitutionally determined cognitive peculiarities might indeed compound the infant's early experience with his caretakers, it is also possible that significant, affectively charged, and repetitive environmental inputs might themselves result in the peculiarities of neural pathways in the neonate's brain. Finally, it is also difficult to distinguish between defects that are primarily inherited and develop as compensatory devices to match the primary defects, and the environmental responses to them (Arieti, 1974).

All this, however, has not eliminated the possibility that genetically transmitted factors contribute to the emergence of the core psychic malformations which might later on result in full-blown schizophrenia. While the concepts of "penetrance" (the frequency with which a genotype becomes manifest) and "expressivity" (the variability in the protophenomenological facets of the genotype) are evoked to salvage a monogenic–biochemical hypothesis (i.e., a single pathological gene being responsible for a specific metabolic error underlying schizophrenia), the emerging consensus leans toward the diathesis–stress theories which note that what is inherited is a predisposition to psychosis not the psychosis itself.

The precise nature of this "predisposition," however, remains unclear. There have been speculations that the infant who is genetically vulnerable in this fashion, is born with a high degree of anxiety, potential for abnormal thought patterns (Karlsson, 1966), and poor visual–proprioceptive integration (Fish and Hagin, 1972). Bleuler (1968), in contrast, believes that what such an infant brings with him is a greater than usual degree of neuropsychological disharmony, an insufficient interplay between different predispositions of his own personality. This genetically determined disharmony not only confounds the environmental input by uneven responses to essentially similar stimuli but is also responsible for the unsteadiness and fragmentation of the subjective response in general. Perhaps it is not an either-or sort of matter. Higher levels of anxiety and vulnerability to unusual thinking might coexist with the Bleularian "disharmony." Other factors might exist as well. There might be a greater degree of constitutionally given aggression and self or other-directed rage in the potentially psychotic organization (H. A. Rosenfeld, 1965). A certain weakness of attachment to objects, a tendency to "react to frustrations with the loss of object relationships"

(Fenichel, 1945, p. 444), and by turning away from the outside world, might also be genetically determined. Together these factors of proneness to anxiety, heightened rage, weakness of object ties, poor frustration tolerance, and vulnerability to abnormal thinking, constitute the "hard-wired" elements of the psychotic core. However, this is only one constituent of the seed of madness. Another major ingredient comes from the dialectical relationship between these temperamental inclinations and the environment into which a child with such potential abnormalities is born.

The Environmental Contribution

The choice of the relatively vague and broad term *environment* in this context is a deliberate one. It is primarily intended to highlight that it is the "environment mother" (Winnicott, 1963, p. 182) rather than the mother as a specific object of desire and fantasy that plays a greater role in the genesis of the infantile psychotic core.[1] Moreover, the use of the term *environment* is aimed at bringing into focus the role of the broader, extrafamilial object world in the perpetuation, if not the origin, of the psychotic core. However, in the earliest phases of infancy and childhood the impact of this larger cosmos too passes through the ever present placenta of maternal care to the child. Hence it is advisable to begin with the earliest role of the mother vis-à-vis her infant.

The most important areas in this realm include the mother's role in (1) facilitation of the infantile cathexis of the object world, restricted in the beginning largely to herself; (2) protecting the infant from excessive stimulation from

[1] Lest this seem like a resurrection of the now disproven concept of "schizophrenogenic mother," I wish to emphasize that there is no implication here of psychopathology in the mother. The compromised maternal functions outlined here might not arise from the mother's own character. These might be the result of the child's unusual temperament, or the mother's lacking libidinal supplies from her husband, or her not having an optimal "holding environment" (Winnicott, 1960) herself in the form of other familial and cultural ego supports.

within and outside and thus laying the structural groundwork for what will later become the "protective shield" (Freud, 1920) of the infant's own ego; and (3) facilitating differentiation on the infant's part by various reciprocal maneuvers including, though not limited to, letting go of the child's body and mind from her omnipotent possession. In the following passages, I will discuss these three areas of mother–child interaction and attempt to show how their derailment contributes to the genesis of the "infantile psychotic self" (Volkan, 1995; see also chapter 1). Following this, I will append some remarks about later influences of the environment at large which will bring in the matter of acquiring ego skills, developing normal or abnormal patterns of thought, and interacting with the extrafamilial object world.

Problematic Object Relations

There is increasing consensus that the human infant arrives in this world in a state of preparedness for bonding, attachment, and object relations (Emde, 1983; Stern, 1985).[2] The human infant from the very beginning shows:

> [A] propensity for participating in eye-to-eye contact; a state responsivity for being activated and soothed by human holding, touching, and rocking; and a propensity for showing prolonged alert attentiveness to the stimulus features contained in the human voice and face [Emde, 1983, p. 171].

At the same time, it is also agreed upon that such hard-wired capacities require environmental input for their optimal unfolding. For instance, the neonate's rooting reflex needs the availability of a feeding mother for its optimal elicitation. Such

---

[2]In the light of contemporary neonatal observational research, the notion of "primary autism" is no longer tenable. There is reasonable consensus about this. Less recognized is a fact that in their introduction to the selected papers of Mahler, Harley and Weil (1979, p. xiii) had already conceded this point by referring to Mahler's autistic phase as "quasi-autistic."

environmental provision (in the not yet distinctly perceived person of the mother) facilitates the establishment of the cathexis of the "mothering principle" (Mahler, 1968, p. 43). The term *mothering principle* here stands for "the perception of, and seeming acceptance of, the relieving ministrations coming from the human partner which, though vague and unspecific, are pleasurable need satisfactions from the mother" (Mahler, 1968, p. 43).

However, these pleasurable satisfactions are contingent upon reliability of maternal care and harmonious mutual cueing between the mother and the child. When the mother is not reliably present to provide such satisfaction to her infant, and when she fails to engage in the feedback loop of mutual cueing with her infant, the latter fails to establish a "libidinal object" (Spitz, 1946). There results an inability to use and subsequently to internalize the mother as a homeostasis assuring object. The baby experiences what Pao has called "pain-in-being-held" and "pain-in-being-laid-down" (1979, p. 153).[3] Such constant distress, with its attendant structural meltdown and emotional inconsolability, becomes the fundamental source of two types of difficulties in object relations.[4]

At the core, there develops a tendency toward readily giving up on object investments and seeking "psychic retreats" (Steiner, 1993) into an autistic haven. This regressive propensity forms the basis in later, adult life of lapses into mindless states, automatonlike experiences, depersonalization, and

[3]Pao's choice of the word *pain* here is significant in light of Freud's (1926) comment that "mental pain"—*seelenschmerz*—is the characteristic reaction to separation when the ego is not clearly distinct from its objects. Pao, after all, is talking here about repeated and traumatic ruptures in maternal care experienced by the infant as agonizing separations.

[4]The failure to establish a libidinal object also interferes with the child's "going-on-being" (Winnicott, 1963, p. 86) and impedes linking his body with his mind. The "psychosomatic existence" (Winnicott, 1960, p. 44) characteristic of an authentic and well-anchored self fails to develop; instead, there is mind–body dissociation with a vulnerability to hypochondria (D. Rosenfeld, 1992) and body image disturbances (see the discussion of related ideas regarding body ego by Lehtonen in chapter 2 of this book).

"psychic blackholes" (Grotstein, 1991) which might, in a secondary defensive move, be "filled" up with bizarre fantasies and, in fortunate circumstances, by creative imagination. Distaste of reality at large, habitual preference of fantasy over reality, a "detached" manner of relating to others, and a passive sort of promiscuity in object relations are other accompaniments of such fundamentally weak object cathexis.

Superimposed on this core defect of object relations is a second, somewhat higher level pattern. This second pattern tends to develop as an upward defense in those individuals who have "stronger constitutions" that permit them to proceed further developmentally or who, after an initial period of unstable maternal care, do receive better libidinal supplies from their mothers or maternal substitutes. This pattern consists of a split "all good" and "all bad" object representation with which corresponding self representations are engaged in an extense affective exchange. Through such reaching up, the potentially psychotic individual approximates the experience of one with a borderline personality organization. However, the former's ego boundaries are diffused and there is marked confusion between which attribute belongs to oneself and which emanates from the surrounding objects. Projective mechanisms, especially when involving malevolent internal objects, lead to the creation of terrifying prosecutors (Volkan and Akhtar, 1979) whom the subject attempts to appease in all kinds of ways; this is the so-called menacing superego of the schizophrenic.

Yet another difficulty arises from the tendency to move toward and simultaneously move away from the external objects. Closeness with objects threatens them with the powerful mobilization of instinctual impulses (both libidinal and aggressive) which, in turn, threatens their brittle ego boundaries. Receiving an electric jolt of anxiety from intimacy, they withdraw only to face new problems. Lacking "object constancy" (Mahler, Pine, and Bergman, 1975), needing a greater "stimulus nutriment" (Rappaport, 1960) to maintain ego functioning, and being unable to hold on to enough "holding introjects" (Adler, 1985), they begin to feel desperately empty and become vulnerable to experiences of near or total non–humanness (Searles, 1960; Singer, 1988). Thus they fluctuate between closeness and distance from objects. Mahler's (1968) "ambitendency," Guntrip's (1969) "in-and-out program," and Burnham, Gladstone, and Gibson's (1969) description of the schizophrenic's "need–fear dilemma" are all concepts that speak to this very matter.

Affective Turbulence

The results of such disastrous mother–infant interactions extend beyond the problematic object relations described above. The infant's affective life is also seriously compromised. Mother's failure to act as a "protective shield" (Freud, 1920) leads the child to experience heavy doses of drive-based stimuli from within and perceptually overwhelming input from outside. Such breeches in the maternal function might be subtle and their impact might turn out to be traumatic only in retrospect (Khan, 1963). More often, it seems that the mother has left her baby in states of "organismic distress" (Mahler, 1968) or "organismic panic" (Mahler et al., 1975; Pao, 1977); that is, the degree of psychophysical terror that the baby cannot relieve without the auxiliary ego support of the mother. Such ruptures of the protective shield or the "skin of the ego" (Bick, 1967; Tustin, 1981) are gross, profoundly traumatic, and cause severe psychic hemorrhage in the form of blurred ego boundaries and pervasive projective mechanisms.

Emotional life under these circumstances lacks in the development of signal affects and their utilization for adaptive purposes. Feelings become all-or-none phenomena that are menacing and unmanageable. A predisposition to panic ensues. Further complication is added by the fact the libido–aggression balance is tilted toward aggression. In Pao's (1979) words, "the fullest development of libidinal potential is

suppressed and the fullest development of aggressive potential is facilitated" (p. 156). Lacking the neutralizing effect of
an adequate libidinal strand and the modulating intervention
of a strong ego, this excessive aggression leads to rampant hatred. At the same time, the child is not permitted outward
expression of this rage. Indeed, the parents convey to the child
that they will fall apart if made the target of this rage. A frequent consequence is the direction of all the hatred toward
one's own mind and body. This self-directed hostility becomes
the reservoir which provides the aggressive fuel for the later
"attacks on linking" (Bion, 1967), including the tendency to
destroy linkages between various thoughts in one's mind.

Yet another peculiarity of affective life is the lack of differentiation among various emotions and between gradations
and intensities of the same emotion. Under average circumstances, the mother empathically tunes in to various emotional
states of her growing child. Her mirroring comments (e.g.,
"Somebody is very happy!") and her executive responses (e.g.,
"Oh! Oh! Let's see what we can do about this.") are calibrated
so as to be as truly reflective of the child's psychic reality as
possible. Thus with qualitatively varying responses and different degrees of quickness or delay of her reactions, the mother
puts the child in touch with a wide gamut of affects and varying levels of drive intensities. Her "naming of affects" (Katan,
1961) is also pertinent here. When all this is missing, as does
tend to happen in the case of an overwhelmed, depressed,
mentally unstable, or otherwise compromised mother (and
later, father), the child's inner affective life remains ill-
discriminated. Emotions continue to exist as unnamed psychophysiological entities, vaguely understood, threatening,
and hence immensely vulnerable to projection.

Inadequate Differentiation

Besides object relations and affective life, the early environment also affects psychic differentiation of the growing child.

Here the term *differentiation* is used in a dual sense. The first sense refers to its usual meaning of the child's increasing sense of being bodily and psychically distinct from the parents (Mahler et al., 1975). The second sense refers to the child's capacity to distinguish between various aspects of his own self while simultaneously keeping them together in a harmonious gestalt (see chapter 3 for clinical material illustrating the failure of this function). The environment conducive to the development of a psychotic core is inoptimally supportive of the child's differentiation in both senses of the word. It might even be nakedly hostile to the child's differentiation. The interpersonal climate in which respect is shown to variable skills, values, and interest is lacking. The "differentiation-impeding parent" (Burnham et al., 1969, p. 48) cannot psychically let go of the child's body (see chapter 6 for a clinical illustration) and treats the child stereotypically, discouraging anything novel, surprising, and spontaneous about the child's behavior. Moreover, all opposition to the parents, including valid opposition, of course, is subtly or overtly discouraged. The child's own perceptions are questioned and invalidated ("No, you do not have a headache!"; "Of course you are hungry. How can you not be hungry?"). All this gaslights the child into believing that he needs his parents constantly to interpret external reality to him:

> [Such a child] is placed in the position of a traveler in a strange country[5] who must depend upon an interpreter to evaluate his encounters with others as well as his performance in these encounters. At best he can venture away from his parents only if he carries with him a mutual guidebook filled

---

[5]The protagonist of Anne Tyler's *The Accidental Tourist* (1985), a writer of tour guides, gives detailed advice to Americans as to where they can get hamburgers, English-language newspapers, and other artifacts of home while they are traveling abroad. Here the parental tendency toward being "overinstructive" seems to have resulted in a socially useful outcome through the intervening processes of identification-with-aggressor and sublimation. However, this is not without exacting a toll upon the hero who himself remains strikingly agorophobic and homebound throughout his life.

with their definitions and rules. The guidebook of social reality imposed by the parents usually is poorly differentiated, rigid and stereotyped, lumping persons into large classes or types rather than distinguishing among varied and different individuals with multiple personality facets. . . . According to the parents' definitions, social interaction is governed by rigid rather than flexible rules and by fixed conceptions of what is acceptable and what is not acceptable [Burnham et al., 1969, pp. 49–50].

However, the dark mosaic of the psychotic core is not restricted to defective object relations, chaotic affective life, and poorly differentiated self and its constituents. There are other problems which originate somewhat later in childhood but nonetheless provide a significant garnish to the already tragically deformed psyche. Prominent among these are (1) deficiencies in basic ego skills; (2) disturbances in thinking; (3) exposure to "unassimilable contradictions" (Burnham et al., 1969, p. 55); and (4) undue parental interference with the child's extrafamilial ties.

Deficient Ego Skills

Acquisition of basic ego skills (ranging from the mundane task of tying shoelaces, for instance, to the complex and multilevel negotiations of interpersonal relationships) depend upon the burgeoning interplay of autonomous ego functions and parental instruction and modeling. Freud's (1923) dictate that "the character of the ego is the precipitate of abandoned object cathexes" (p. 29) is applicable to the identifications which ensue from the above mentioned interplay and which, in turn, enrich the ego's behavioral repertoire. When instruction aimed at imparting skills is given by the parents in an atmosphere of tension, resentment, and participatory half-heartedness, the child learns only superficially or fails to learn altogether. Moreover, if the necessary patience on the parent's part is missing, there is a pressure on the child to learn and "get on with it," become quickly independent. This renders acquisition of ego skills tantamount to abandonment by the parents in the child's mind and thus contaminates an otherwise desirable goal with malignant consequences; many negative therapeutic reactions in the course of therapy during later, adult life emanate from this dynamic substrate (Gruenert, 1979; Akhtar, 1992b). Weakness of ego skills also impedes role-taking capacity necessary for learning, and a vicious cycle is established where the two impairments reinforce each other.

Thought Disturbances

Thought disturbances originate from the intense self-directed aggression which inwardly mutilates the fabric of thinking. Propensity toward loss of object cathexis also adds to thought disturbance by creating states of thought blocking and mindlessness. A family atmosphere infused by "double-bind" (Bateson, Jackson, Haley, and Weakland, 1956) communication pattern further interferes with coherent and reliable thinking. For instance, when an enraged parent yells at the child, "But I have told you not to listen to me when I am angry!" the child is left totally perplexed. How is he to interpret this message? He is damned no matter what he does. Another example is when a father, while assigning a task to a child, adds, "but I know that you most likely will not do it." Again, the child is trapped. If he accomplishes the task, he has shown the father's prediction to be incorrect and thus has hurt him. And, if he does not, he has proven the father right but disappointed him by not doing the task! Such a child can be certain of very little about his own and other's thinking except that it is all very confusing. Wynne, Ryckoff, Day, and Hirsch (1958), Wynne and Singer (1963), and Lidz (1963) have further elaborated and described additional patterns of such transmission of irrationality from parents to children.

In contrast to these theorists, Kafka (1989) holds that exposure to ambiguity and multiple realities regarding any event actually has a positive impact upon the growing child's capacity to think meaningfully. He proposes that it is an *underexposure* to paradox—necessarily involving "different levels of abstraction that are not immediately apparent" (p. 38)—that robs the child of the capacity to view events from multiple perspectives. Kafka traces the resulting rigidity of thinking to parental intolerance of ambiguity, often revealed by the tenacity with which they maintain the family myths. Such parents insist upon unrealistically clear thinking and do not allow their children to "indulge without danger in the richness of blending and other ambiguous experiences" (p. 47). Conceptual inflexibility on the part of the parents also impedes the child's individuation since individuation necessarily involves both continuities and discontinuities from the parental psychic realities (see also Poland, 1977; Akhtar, 1992b).

Unassimilable Contradictions

This brings up the issue of the child being exposed to "unassimilable contradictions" (Burnham et al., 1969, p. 55). Such contradictions might exist within a single parent, between two parents, or between the parents and the extrafamilial world. Intraparental contradictions, though not entirely independent of the child's own drive and fantasy contributions (e.g., "good" and "bad" mother of early infancy, the madonna–whore split of oedipal phase), in this context, refer to the actual presence of markedly contradictory behaviors on a parent's part which makes it difficult for a child to establish a coherent image of that parent in his mind. For instance, a parent might convey to the child that he is to remain utterly dependent and yet serve as a source of libidinal supplies for the parent. Or, he or she might act in an extremely generous manner one day and in an equally intense withholding, miserly manner the next day. Similar contradictions might exist on an interparental basis. One parent might encourage assertiveness and the other compliance. One parent might nourish dependence and the other facilitate independence. Contradictions might also exist between the familial expectations and those emanating from the outer world. The degree of autonomy, assertiveness, self-expression, competitiveness, novelty seeking, and authenticity encouraged by the family and the outside world might differ. While this gap is perhaps existent for most families, it is more marked in families of preschizophrenics which are often idiosyncratic in their norms, geographically isolated, and prone to inculcate xenophobia in their offspring.

Deficient Extrafamilial Input

This last mentioned tendency most directly interferes with the child's ability to develop extrafamilial object relations. He is thus deprived of potential sources of additional libidinal supplies and acquisition of ego skills through later, selective identifications. Moreover, such insular existence also robs the child of the corrective and compensatory influence that a chance at developing object relations outside of the parental orbit might otherwise provide.

The Role of Fantasy

The emphasis upon the constitutional vulnerabilities and the environmental failures should not give an impression that the child's own fantasy life[6] plays no role in the assemblage of the psychotic core. The fact is that all the above-mentioned ego defects (whether constitutionally or environmentally

---

[6]The emphasis upon the child's intrapsychic life here should not lead one to overlook that malevolent parental fantasies might also enter, at times, with considerable force, in the mangled tissue of the child's psychotic core (Searles, 1965; Volkan, 1995; see also the chapters by Volkan and Apprey in the present book).

caused) affect the form and content of the child's phase-specific fantasies as the epigenetic program of psychosexual development unfolds. Emanating from a matrix of intense aggression and a splitting and projection-prone ego, oral, anal, and phallic–oedipal scenarios acquire truly fantastic qualities. Biting becomes gory cannibalism, spitting creates an ocean. Defecation leads to defiling the entire world, and anal withholding can stop the slightest movement of thought lest it "leak" out. Oedipal conflicts too are inordinately aggressivized. On the one hand, this might result in intense castration anxiety and highly unrealistic visions of vagina dentata and the phallic woman in males, and equally terrifying images of a poisonous and violently penetrating penis in females. On the other hand, a defensive flight into idealization might lead to an exaggerated estimation of heterosexual love in the positive oedipal relations and of homosexual love in the negative oedipal relations. Splitting might perpetuate the madonna–whore compartmentalization in the mind and projective identification might lead to a constant confusion between the oedipal victor and the excluded losing party.

Such distortions and fantastic exaggerations, however, are not only fantasy accompaniments of the psychotic core. Its other features include "bizarre objects" (Bion, 1967) and retrospective fantasy elaboration of preverbal defects in the psychic structure. Bizarre objects result from the vicious hatred directed against the self and its internalized objects. The attack on one's mental processes (accentuated by a developmentally later inversion of the envious attack on the parental coupling and linkage) destroys the inner percepts of objects.

[The mechanisms of splitting, repudiation, and projective identification] then splinter and fragment the part objects and violently send off into space the dismembered fragments of part objects with splintered parts of mind within them so as to rid the remaining psyche of them. This leads to the formation of bizarre objects which then, after their projected territory, boomerang and cluster in an eerie, bizarre, orbital screen around the impoverished self which is even more confused by the evacuation and projection of its own contents [Grotstein, 1977, p. 431].

Retrospective fantasies are also created by the perceptually bashful, energically weak, and affectively unstable ego. Focus of such fantasies is usually upon the extensive debris of the troubled preverbal period of life. These fantasies frequently have a pseudospiritual bent and involve the cosmic themes of birth and death, the "clever baby" (Ferenczi, 1923), reincarnation, and other such religious and supernatural motifs.

Concluding Remarks

In keeping with the spirit of this book, the foregoing survey of literature highlights the point that the constituents of the psychotic core are indeed multifaceted. It takes into account the role of constitutional factors, the environmental input, and the dialectical play between them. As a result, it implores one to consider not only the influence of the environment upon the child but also the reaction of the environment to a child with constitutional peculiarities. Not to be overlooked is the additional role of intrapsychic fantasy of the child as well as that of the parents insofar as the latter too affect the psychic unfolding of the child. The separation of these intricately related factors (summarized in Table 8.1) in the foregoing discussion is merely an accommodation to didactic necessity. The fact is that there is much ebb and flow between the dynamic processes generated by constitution, early environment, the child's intrapsychic constructions, and the fantasies of the parents.

Moving a step further, one also has to take into account that the formation of a psychotic core is not tantamount to

TABLE 8.1
Constituents of the Psychotic Core

I. *Heredity and Constitutional Factors*

Excessive anxiety
Excessive rage
Potential for abnormal thinking
Impaired visual–proprioceptive integration
Weak object cathexis
Neuropsychological disharmony

II. *Environmental Contribution*

Problematic object relations and psychosomatic dissociation
Affective turbulence
Inadequate differentiation including body image disturbances
Deficient ego skills
Thought disturbance
Unassimilable contradictions
Xenophobia and deficient extrafamilial input

III. *The Role of Intrapsychic Fantasy*

Intense, split, and fantastic phase specific scenarios
Retrospective fantasizing
Bizarre objects
Incorporation of malevolent parental fantasies

the development, in later adult life, of a full-blown psychosis. To the contrary, the psychotic core can have a variety of outcomes which range from those compatible with seeming normality to focal or generalized takeover of the ego by psychotic processes and their manifestations (see chapter 1 for details). The former possibility, of course, involves an "encapsulation" (D. Rosenfeld, 1992; Volkan, 1995) of the psychotic core. This can take many forms. Freud's (1940) description of ego splitting whereby contact with reality coexists with psychotic thinking, and Bion's (1967) delineation of the coexistence of psychotic and nonpsychotic sectors of the personality, are pertinent in this context (see also Salonen's chapter in the present book). When such encapsulation is subterranean and patched over by seemingly neurotic mechanisms, it can pose considerable diagnostic and therapeutic difficulties. The "as-if" personality described by Deutsch (1942) belongs to this category. Such individuals display a tendency to rapidly identify with others, an easily shifting morality, an automatonlike suggestibility, and defensive repudiation of aggression, lending to them an air of negative goodness and mild amiability. In relatively classical analytic treatment the deeper pathology of such individuals is often overlooked.

> [In such cases,] the psychoanalyst may collude for years with the patient's need to be psychoneurotic (as opposed to "mad") and to be treated as psychoneurotic. The analysis goes well, and everyone is pleased. The only drawback is that the analysis never ends. It can be terminated, and the patient may even mobilize a psychoneurotic false self for the purpose of finishing and expressing gratitude. But, in fact, the patient knows that there has been no change in the underlying (psychotic) state and the analyst and the patient have succeeded in colluding to bring about a failure [Winnicott, 1971, p. 102].

This brings up the issue of treatment of individuals with a psychotic core sharply into focus. Clearly, the treatment needs to take into account the multifaceted determinants of their psychotic core, regardless of whether it chooses to mobilize this core in the transferential here-and-now or palliatively buttress the defenses against the breakthrough of the deeper substrate. To begin with, then, the treatment approach needs to be biopsychosocial since the fundamental nature of this pathology is biopsychosocial. Pharmacologic and social interventions therefore deserve a place of importance in the treatment approach. At the same time, it cannot be overlooked that these modalities are most effective only when psychotherapeutic help is available on an ongoing basis.

> [Moreover, there might even be] clinical evidence to show that certain schizophrenic patients who do not respond to psychopharmacological treatment may be receptive to a

psychotherapeutic approach, if they present at least a certain degree of integration of their personality, a capacity for differentiated object relations within the psychotic regression, at least normal intelligence, and an absence of antisocial features [Kernberg, 1992, p. vii].

Ideally such a psychotherapeutic approach should attempt to integrate the conflict–deficit, interpretation–holding, insight–empathy dichotomies rampant in our field. The therapeutic stance derived from such an integration is an optimal synthesis of the "classic" and "romantic" visions (Strenger, 1989) of psychoanalysis. From the "classic" side, such a therapeutic approach receives its emphasis upon analyzing the role that splitting and projective identification play in reducing the patient's capacity for thinking and for a coherent self-experience. Moreover, interpretive efforts are directed toward transforming bizarre and confusional phenomena into more organized states, betraying the primitive splitting of object relations into their idealized and denigrated caricatures (Searles, 1965; H. A. Rosenfeld, 1965; D. Rosenfeld, 1992; Volkan, 1976). From the "romantic" side, the therapeutic approach derives its regard for the patient's need for deep regression (Khan, 1983; Little, 1990) and a "corrective symbiotic experience" (Pao, 1979) through which the patient can make up his inner deficiency and experience a psychic "rebirth" (Adler, 1985, p. 157). It is only through such a synthesis of the two visions of psychoanalysis that one achieves a true loyalty to the clinical material above and beyond the commitment to one or the other theoretical paradigm. Such informed eclecticism coupled with the deep informative potential and containing function of the analyst's countertransference (Searles, 1965; Boyer, 1978, 1994; Pao, 1979; D. Rosenfeld, 1992; see also chapters 5 through 7 of this book) yields the most helpful approach to treating the anguish associated with a psychotic core to the personality. In the end, it is not a question of genetic vulnerability or environmental failure or intrapsychic fantasy either in understanding psychopathology or in its amelioration. All three aspects have to be taken into account. Clearly, it is our hope that this book will highlight, refine, and emphatically convey this message.

References

Adler, G. (1985), *Borderline Psychopathology and its Treatment.* Northvale, NJ: Jason Aronson.

Akhtar, S. (1992a), *Broken Structures: Severe Personality Disorders and Their Treatment.* Northvale, NJ: Jason Aronson.

—— (1992b), Tethers, orbits, and invisible fences: Clinical, developmental, sociocultural, and technical aspects of optimal distance. In: *When the Body Speaks: Psychological Meanings in Kinetic Clues,* ed. S. Kramer & S. Akhtar. Northvale, NJ: Jason Aronson, pp. 21–57.

Arieti, S. (1974), *Interpretation of Schizophrenia.* New York: Basic Books.

Bateson, G., Jackson, D. D., Haley, J., & Weakland, J. (1956), Toward a theory of schizophrenia. *Behavioral Science,* 1:251–264.

Bick, E. (1967), The experience of the skin in early object relations. *Internat. J. Psycho-Anal.,* 49:484–486.

Bion, W. R. (1967), *Second Thoughts.* London: Heinemann.

—— (1957), Differentiation of the psychotic from the non-psychotic personalities. *Internat. J. Psycho-Anal.,* 38:266–275.

Bleuler, M. (1968), A twenty-three year longitudinal study of 208 schizophrenics and impressions in regard to the nature of schizophrenia. In: *The Transmission of Schizophrenia,* ed. D. Rosenthal & S. S. Kety. London: Pergammon Press, pp 3–12.

Boyer, L. B. (1978), Countertransference experiences in working with severely regressed patients. *Contemp. Psychoanal.,* 14:48–72.

—— (1994), Countertransference: Condensed history and personal view of issues with regressed patients. *J. Psychother. Pract. & Res.,* 3:122–137.

Burnham, D. L., Gladstone, A. E., & Gibson, R. W. (1969), *Schizophrenia and the Need–Fear Dilemma.* New York: International Universities Press.

Deutsch, H. (1942), Some forms of emotional disturbance and their relationship to schizophrenia. *Psychoanal. Quart.,* 11:301–321.

Emde, R. N. (1983), The pre-representational self and its affective core. *The Psychoanalytic Study of the Child.* New Haven, CT: Yale University Press, 38:165–192.

Fenichel, O. (1945), *The Psychoanalytic Theory of Neurosis.* New York: W. W. Norton.

Ferenczi, S. (1923), The dream of the "clever baby." In: *Further Contributions to the Theory and Technique of Psychoanalysis.* London: Hogarth Press, 1950, pp. 349–350.

Fish, B., & Hagin, R. (1972), Visual–motor disorders in infants at risk for schizophrenia. *Arch. Gen. Psychiatry,* 27:594–600.

Freud, S. (1920), Beyond the Pleasure Principle. *Standard Edition,* 18:1–64. London: Hogarth Press, 1955.

——— (1923), The Ego and the Id. *Standard Edition,* 19:1–59. London: Hogarth Press, 1961.

——— (1926), Inhibitions, Symptoms and Anxiety. *Standard Edition,* 20:75–172. London: Hogarth Press, 1959.

——— (1940), An outline of psychoanalysis. *Standard Edition,* 23:139–207. London: Hogarth Press, 1964.

Gottesman, I. I., & Shields, J. (1966), Contributions of twin studies to perspectives on schizophrenia. In: *Progress in Experimental Personality Research,* Vol. 3, ed. B. A. Maher. New York: Academy Press, pp. 1–84.

Grotstein, J. (1977), The psychoanalytic concept of schizophrenia: II—Reconciliation. *Internat. J. Psycho-Anal.,* 58:427–452.

——— (1991), Nothingness, meaninglessness, chaos, and the "black hole": III—Self regulation and the background presence of primary identification. *Contemp. Psychoanal.,* 27:1–33.

Gruenert, U. (1979), The negative therapeutic reaction as a reactivation of a disturbed process of separation in transference. *Bull. Euro. Psychoanal. Fed.,* 16:5–9.

Guntrip, H. (1969), *Schizoid Phenomena, Object Relations and the Self.* New York: International Universities Press.

Harley, M., & Weil, A. (1979), Introduction. In: *The Selected Papers of Margaret S. Mahler,* Vol. 1. New York: Jason Aronson, pp. ix–xx.

Kafka, J. (1989), *Multiple Realities in Clinical Practice.* New Haven, CT: Yale University Press.

Karlsson, J. L. (1966), *The Biologic Basis of Schizophrenia.* Springfield, IL: Charles Thomas.

Katan, A. (1961), Some thoughts about the role of verbalization in early childhood. *The Psychoanalytic Study of the Child,* 16:184–188. New York: International Universities Press.

Kernberg, O. F. (1984), *Severe Personality Disorders: Psychotherapeutic Strategies.* New Haven, CT: Yale University Press.

——— (1992), Foreword. In: *The Psychotic Aspects of the Personality,* by D. Rosenfeld. London: Karnac Books, pp. vii–xiii.

Kety, S. S., Rosenthal, D., Wender, P. H., & Schulsinger, F. (1968), The types and prevalence of mental illness in the biological and adoptive families of adoptive schizophrenics. In: *The Transmission of Schizophrenia,* ed. D. Rosenthal & S. S. Kety. London: Pergammon Press, pp. 345–362.

——— ——— ——— ——— (1971), A program of research on heredity in schizophrenia. *Behav. Sci.,* 16:191–201.

——— ——— ——— ——— (1975), Mental illness in biological and adoptive families of adopted individuals who have become schizophrenic: A preliminary report based on psychiatric interviews. In: *Genetic Research in Psychiatry,* ed. R. R. Fiev, D. Rosenthal, & H. Brill. Baltimore: Johns Hopkins University Press, pp. 147–165.

Khan, M. M. R. (1963), The concept of cumulative trauma. In: *The Privacy of the Self*. New York: International Universities Press, pp. 42–58.
———— (1983), *Hidden Selves: Between Theory and Practice in Psychoanalysis*. New York: International Universities Press.
Kringlen, E. (1967), *Heredity and Environment in the Functional Psychoses: An Epidemiological–Clinical Twin Study*. London: Heinemann.
Lidz, T. (1973), *On the Origin and Treatment of Schizophrenic Disorders*. New York: Basic Books.
Little, M. I. (1990), *Psychotic Anxieties and Containment*. Northvale, NJ: Jason Aronson.
Mahler, M. S. (1968), *On Human Symbiosis and the Vicissitudes of Individuation*. New York: International Universities Press.
Mahler, M. S., Pine, F., & Bergman, A. (1975), *The Psychological Birth of the Human Infant*. New York: Basic Books.
Pao, P. N. (1977), On the formation of schizophrenic symptoms. *Internat. J. Psycho-Anal.*, 58:389–401.
———— (1979), *Schizophrenic Disorders: Theory and Treatment from a Psychodynamic Point of View*. New York: International Universities Press.
Poland, W. S. (1977), Pilgrimage: Action and tradition in self-analysis. *J. Amer. Psychoanal. Assn.*, 25:399–416.
Rappaport, D. (1960), The Structure of Psychoanalytic Theory. *Psycholog. Issues*, Monogr. 6. New York: International Universities Press.
Rosenfeld, D. (1992), *The Psychotic Aspects of the Personality*. London: Karnac Books.
Rosenfeld, H. A. (1965), *Psychotic States: A Psychoanalytic Approach*. London: Hogarth Press.
Rosenthal, D. (1975), The genetics of schizophrenia. In: *American Handbook of Psychiatry*, Vol. 3, ed. S. Arieti & E. B. Brody. New York: Basic Books, pp. 588–600.
———— Kety, S. S. (1968), *The Transmission of Schizophrenia*. London: Pergamon Press.
Searles, H. F. (1960), *The Non-Human Environment in Normal Development and in Schizophrenia*. New York: International Universities Press.
———— (1965), *Collected Papers on Schizophrenia and Related Subjects*. New York: International Universities Press.
Singer, M. (1988), Fantasy or structural defect: The borderline dilemma as viewed from analysis of an experience of non-humanness. *J. Amer. Psychoanal. Assn.*, 36:31–59.
Spitz, R. A. (1946), Anaclitic depression: An inquiry into the genesis of psychiatric conditions in early childhood. *The Psychoanalytic Study of the Child*. New York: International Universities Press, 2:313–342.
Steiner, J. (1993), *Psychic Retreats: Pathological Organizations in Psychotic, Neurotic, and Borderline Patients*. London: Karnac Books.
Stern, B. N. (1985), *The Interpersonal World of the Infant*. New York: Basic Books.
Strenger, C. (1989), The classic and the romantic visions in psychoanalysis. *Internat. J. Psycho-Anal.*, 70:595–610.

Tienari, P. (1968), Schizophrenia in monozygotic male twins. In: *The Transmission of Schizophrenia*, ed. D. Rosenthal & S. S. Kety. London: Pergamon Press, pp. 27–36.

――― (1991), The interaction between genetic vulnerability and family environment: The Finnish adoptive family study of schizophrenia. *Acta Psychiatr. Scand.*, 84:460–465.

Tustin, F. (1981), *Autistic States in Children*. London: Tavistock Press.

Tyler, A. (1985), *Accidental Tourist*. New York: Knopf.

Volkan, V. D. (1976), *Primitive Internalized Object Relations*. New York: International Universities Press.

――― (1995), *The Infantile Psychotic Self and Its Fates*. Northvale, NJ: Jason Aronson.

Volkan, V. D., & Akhtar, S. (1979), The symptoms of schizophrenia: Contributions of the structural theory and object relations theory. In: *Integrating Ego Psychology and Object Relations Theory*, ed. L. Seretsky, G. D. Goldman, & D. S. Milman. Dubuque, Iowa: Kendall/Hunt, pp. 270–285.

Wender, P. H., Rosenthal, D., Kety, S. S., Schulsinger, F., & Welner, J. (1974), Cross-fostering: A research strategy for clarifying the role of genetic and experiential factors in the etiology of schizophrenia. *Arch. Gen. Psychiatry*, 30:121–128.

Winnicott, D. W. (1960), The theory of parent–infant relationship. In: *The Maturational Processes and the Facilitating Environment*. New York: International Universities Press, 1965, pp. 37–55.

――― (1963), From dependence towards independence in the development of the individual. In: *The Maturational Processes and the Facilitating Environment*. New York: International Universities Press, 1965, pp. 83–92.

――― (1965), *The Maturational Processes and the Facilitating Environment*. New York: International Universities Press.

――― (1971), *Playing and Reality*. Harmondsworth, U.K.: Penguin Books.

Wynne, L. C., Ryckoff, I., Day, J., and Hirsch, S. (1958), Pseudo-mutuality in the family relations of schizophrenics. *Psychiatry*, 21:205–220.

――― Singer, M. T. (1963), Thought disorder and family relations of schizophrenics: I—A research strategy. *Arch. Gen. Psychiatry*, 9:191–198.

Name Index

Subject Index

Accidental Tourist, The (Tyler),
  188n
Adult psychotic self, 12
Affects
  bad, 7
  good, 6–8
  neurobiological effects of,
    32–33
  perceptions and, 48–49
  primal repression and, 41
  related to Isakower phenom-
    enon, 33–37
  turbulence of, 186–187
  vital versus categorical, 35–36
Ambiguity, 190–191
Ambitendency, 186
Anal sadism, 117
Analyst
  cultural influences on experi-
    ences of, 159–160
  mental set of, 159
  nonintrusive, 161
  personal experiences of, 158
  reverie of, 162

Analytic frame, 156–157
Anorexia, 108
Anxiety
  internalization of, 144, 149–150
  signal, 74
As-if personality, 196
Atrocities, as intrapsychic
  adaptation, 75–78
Attachment, preparedness for,
  183–184
Autistic encapsulation, 9
Autonomy, 73

Bad feelings, 138, 148, 151
Biology, in mad seed develop-
  ment, 12–15
Birth process, changes with,
  22–23
Bizarre objects, 193–194
  transforming of, 197
Blank state, 38–39
Bodily symptoms, 144–145
  of infantile psychotic self,
    133–136